# THE TECHNIQUE OF PHOTOGRAPHING BIRDS

*The Technique of*

# PHOTOGRAPHING
# BIRDS

*by*

JOHN WARHAM
*A.R.P.S., M.B.O.U.*

**THE FOCAL PRESS**

**LONDON AND NEW YORK**

*First published in 1956*

Printed in Great Britain
by W. & J. Mackay & Co. Ltd, Chatham

# Contents

# *Illustrations*

7

# Introduction

THE GROWING POPULARITY of outdoor pursuits and the wider interest taken in natural history in recent years has inevitably been reflected in photography; today more and more people are using their cameras to show plants, insects and animals. Apart from Man himself, few living things have been studied more closely than have birds, and bird photographs predominate in the nature sections of photographic exhibitions just as bird books outnumber those devoted to other aspects of wild life. This is, after all, an understandable situation; for birds, unlike many animals and insects, are abroad by day and not only are they found in all countries and climates, but they positively command attention by their activities, by their songs and by their varied colours.

This book has been written for the guidance of photographers wishing to tackle the portrayal of wild birds in their natural surroundings. The approach throughout is a practical one; the work is intended to act both as a training manual and a reference book, and it is hoped that it may help the reader past some of the more usual obstacles of which all beginners in this field fall foul during their initial attempts. A knowledge of elementary darkroom procedure has been presumed. The illustrations have been carefully selected to demonstrate certain aspects of technique; there are few pictures here which do not tell a story.

The standard to which the reader is invited to aim is a high one. Too often birds are regarded by photographers as extremely difficult subjects and people tend to regard any picture of a bird, however crude, as praiseworthy. But the truth is that many species may be easily photographed provided the cameraman uses the

9

correct methods; out of focus pictures, or those with detail blurred by camera shake or subject movement, usually deserve no commendation.

Throughout this book there is an insistence on putting the interests of the bird before the needs of photography. This is particularly important when working at a nesting site, for here the photographer is taking advantage of the bird's parental instincts, and carelessness or lack of consideration can be disastrous to the young ones. Only by an honest regard for his subject's welfare can the bird photographer make sure that his activities do not interfere with successful breeding. It is partly because the bird must have first consideration that so much preliminary work is necessary before the camera can be brought into use. Bitter experience over countless generations has influenced birds in populated countries to avoid human beings; the very survival of many species depends on their innate wariness. Sometimes much hard work may be needed to overcome this timidity and it is a capacity for hard work rather than an abundance of patience that is the essential need of a good bird photographer. Birds living in places where Man is seldom seen, as in the polar regions, show little fear; to such, Man is not a normal hazard, so that one can walk into a penguin rookery, for example, without causing a mass exodus of the birds from their nests; indeed, the visitor is more likely to be discouraged from a close approach by the threatening lunges of pointed bills. In such areas bird photography can be undertaken without the need for concealment; at home, on the other hand, confidence is only gained gradually. The photographer who tries to rush his fences often takes a fall and his subjects suffer from his over-eagerness.

Bird photography need not be an expensive hobby. Perhaps material costs run a little higher than in other branches of photography, for there are inevitably a certain number of exposures that are spoiled by subject movement. One can, of course, spend a good deal of money on useful though non-essential items which probably only come into their own on isolated occasions. For getting about a car is a great boon and it enables one's field of action to be greatly widened. Yet even a bicycle has its advantages, especially where the distance between home and the working area is short. And on a bicycle one can proceed down the narrowest of lanes where a vehicle would be unable to follow.

Perhaps bird photography is a stimulating pastime because it satisfies Man's primitive urge to pursue a quarry, and in one way or another a great many people derive pleasure from pitting their wits against shy and elusive creatures like birds. Thus the birdsman's pictures are his trophies of the chase. Many workers aim at producing fine portraits of their subjects, but now that most European birds have been so well photographed there seems a definite tendency for the camera to be used to show behaviour seldom or never before recorded on film; in such fields there is room for a great deal of original work. Elsewhere, particularly in South America, Africa, Asia, and here in Australia there are endless possibilities for the bird photographer to break new ground. All over the world photography is playing its part in increasing the man-in-the-street's awareness of the wild life around him, thereby helping to influence local opinion so that in the face of the shrinkage of forests, swamps and other natural refuges, the conservationist may be able to save for posterity many species now threatened with extinction.

Albany,
West Australia.
1956.

*The writer would like to acknowledge his indebtedness to the various people who have directly or indirectly assisted in the preparation of this book. To many landowners both in Britain and elsewhere without whose help few bird photographers can pursue their hobby adequately, and to those fellow-workers both from Europe and overseas who have sent some of their best photographs for reproduction here. Thanks are also due to Cmdr. A. W. P. Robertson for details of his mobile hide, and to Mr. O. W. Bingham who has built, maintained and improved the electronic flash equipment with which many of my own pictures were made.*

12

# The Choice of Equipment

THE NATURE PHOTOGRAPHER's main problem when dealing with wild birds in their natural environment is how to counter their innate shyness. Such shyness generally makes it impossible to get the camera close enough without the use of some method of concealment in a place to which birds regularly resort. Even then the camera can only be brought to within a limited distance from the bird; there is inevitably some noise associated with the operation of any make of camera and most birds are readily frightened by strange sounds. This means in practice that with rather small subjects like these, the permissible working distances only enable correspondingly small images to be produced when lenses of medium focal length are used. To get the birds large enough on the negatives to reveal adequate detail on printing and enlargement usually necessitates lenses of longer focal length than are employed for general photography.

Because birds are such independent creatures a great many pictures are taken of them at their nests. When nesting they are more approachable, more tolerant of casual noises, and the photographer has a good idea of where to train his camera so that, all in all, his chances of getting successful pictures are greatly increased. But the very fact that he takes advantage of his subject's parental instincts sets him another problem—he must so conduct his operations that he does not prejudice successful nesting. Thus cameras which are noisy in operation, whether due to the shutter (the commonest source of trouble), the film winding mechanism, or any other cause, are unsuitable for this kind of close-up work unless these disadvantages can be eradicated in some way.

13

Although the camera may be trained on a nest or some other point to which the bird is expected to return, it is frequently impossible to be sure just where it will be when the opportunity for making an exposure occurs. The bird may stand slightly to one side of the field covered by the lens, and while the bird is there it is impossible to move the camera to point in the right direction for it will detect the movement and depart in panic. Thus, not only is a fairly large image desirable but the negative should also include a good deal of the surroundings as well. The greater the area included the greater the chances of securing a picture; most bird studies are the result of enlarging only part of the negative.

Cameras have to be considered in the light of these special problems as regards their suitability or otherwise for bird work. Here, as in other departments of photography, it is not merely the camera used but the skill and imagination of the person handling it that determines the quality of the final result. There is no one camera which is ideal in every respect; certain types excel for certain aspects of bird photography and several kinds are capable of yielding first-class results; some are quite unsuitable.

### Folding Cameras

The general run of $2\frac{1}{4} \times 3\frac{1}{4}$ in. and $2\frac{1}{4} \times 2\frac{1}{4}$ in. folding cameras have lenses of too short a focal length to be of much use for bird photography unless one is working with big birds like swans, geese or pelicans. The lenses are fixed and the bellows extension limited so that the fitting of a longer focus lens is usually impracticable. I have a camera in this category in my kit—a Super Ikonta which is mainly used for record shots, such as pictures of habitats, and hides. Sometimes it proves handy for making flight studies in daylight, and particularly for showing flocks of birds wheeling above their nesting colonies or roosting sites. And I have occasionally used it for flight shots of birds at close quarters in conjunction with electronic flash. When a bird is in flight it offers a much bigger subject than when at rest so that a larger image is obtained on the negative.

## Miniature Cameras

Few serious bird photographers in Britain rely solely on miniature cameras, though on the Continent the 35 mm. outfit is more often used than here. With the miniature two points previously mentioned crop up—the problem of shutter noise (most acute with focal plane shutters) and the need to use a longer focus lens, often a telephoto, to boost up the image to enable satisfactory enlargements to be made. The lenses of 40–50 mm. focal length usually fitted are unsuitable, for the camera can never be brought closer than 3½ feet and the average subject is too small at this distance for satisfactory results. 35 mm. cameras of this type, fitted with non-interchangeable lenses, are therefore unsuitable for the present purpose. But there are a number of cameras having interchangeable lenses fitting on to a shutter of the sector type— nowadays usually a Compur or Prontor—and these are quite suitable for taking birds. Some of these cameras are reasonably priced and are made to take lenses of various focal lengths up to about 9 cm.

I have deliberately emphasized the desirability of the shutter being of the sector type, since many top-grade miniatures are equipped with efficient but too often noisy focal plane shutters. Modern sector shutters are by no means silent, but they are generally sufficiently so for bird work provided care is taken. But many focal plane shutters are too noisy to be practicable. Of course some birds will become so indifferent to sounds from within a hide that they would not be scared by a press camera. But the bird worker needs an outfit suitable for all the varied temperaments he will find in his volatile subjects; he must be able to photograph both bold and nervous sitters. Using a powerful telephoto so that the camera can be set well back from the nest is hardly the answer; a bird scared of a sound at five feet will still be scared at fifteen feet, for its hearing is better than ours.

The only feasible alternative seems to be to fit a Compur or Prontor shutter behind the lens, or to fit a lens already mounted in a sectional shutter of this type. With some cameras this may only mean using an adapter ring; but more often the work will have to be done by a competent camera mechanic, for the alteration must be made in such a way that the added lens gives sharp images within the range of movements possible from the focusing mount. Certain types of camera in this category might even be fitted with a behind-lens "silent" shutter of the kind described later in this chapter, and such an adaptation would enable the miniature to be used at close quarters with little danger of scaring the quarry.

Such alterations call for some modification of usual focusing practice. With coupled rangefinder cameras the rangefinder cannot be employed when an additional shutter has been fitted. And with non-rangefinder types, focusing by the scale on the lens mount cannot be done unless the lens has been fitted so that the original calibration is correct; otherwise the mount must be rescaled. Focusing is simplified if the camera has a focusing back— these are made to fit several types of precision miniatures. Alternatively, with some makes, a reflex housing can be used for focusing with telephoto lenses.

The 35 mm. reflex camera adapted to take a sectional shutter in front of the mirror and in conjunction with a telephoto is quite suitable for much of the bird worker's subjects, for focusing is done visually and is positive; care must be taken to ensure that the additional shutter does not carry the lens too far forward, otherwise only near objects will be sharp. One drawback here is that as the sectional shutter is now in front of the mirror, the camera can only be used as a reflex while the front shutter is open; once the subject has been focused the mirror must be set in the "up" position and the focal plane shutter left fully open while the sectional shutter is being used. Some 35 mm. reflexes can also be fitted with focusing backs or prismatic eye-level viewers, and these will be found very useful when working within a hide, where head room is limited.

The miniature camera will appeal particularly to those who aim to make colour transparencies of birds for viewing by projection. Owing to the good depths of field given, comparatively wide apertures and fairly fast shutter speeds are possible, and this both widens the field of potential subjects and helps to cut down film

16

wastage through movement. The film itself is considerably cheaper per exposure, both for colour and for black-and-white, than when larger size material is employed.

35 mm. cameras may also be used successfully for making colour studies of birds by electronic flash. Portable high-speed outfits are not usually powerful enough unless the lens is opened up to about $f4.5$ to $f6.3$, and this means that with a quarter-plate outfit the depth of field is very shallow. But with a miniature the situation is much better and quite successful pictures can be made even at apertures of this order. With electronic flash wastage due to movement of the subject during the exposure is eliminated, so that even flight studies in full colour may be obtained with careful handling. Telephoto-equipped coupled-rangefinder miniatures are also ideal for flight shots in daylight.

An increasing number of bird photographers use a 35 mm. camera for colour work while still retaining their bigger outfits for black and white, or for making the larger colour transparencies for reproduction.

Despite the miniature camera's versatility it has certain practical disadvantages. First, the bird photographer who wishes to produce negatives good enough to make exhibition prints of the usual 20 × 16 in. size will be hard-pressed to succeed using a miniature. The reason is that while a 35 mm. negative can certainly produce a 20 × 16 in. print showing adequate detail, this is usually only possible by a combination of careful technique and enlargement of the whole of the negative area. Unfortunately, with such wayward creatures as birds, the subject is often not in the correct position on the negative to make an attractive or satisfactory enlargement from the whole of it.

On the other hand not everyone wishes to produce such large prints, and those who are satisfied with a 10 × 8 in. picture should be able to produce many satisfactory photographs with a suitable miniature. And if he is mainly interested in birds rather than photography—that is if he is a photographically-inclined ornithologist rather than an ornithologically-inclined photographer— the right kind of miniature may be ideal for making the record shots he requires, and for taking series depicting different facets of behaviour, where exhibition quality prints are neither called for nor expected. The lever-wind method of film transport customary with modern miniatures is also an advantage when a number of shots are required in quick succession.

### Reflex Cameras

A popular type of single lens reflex camera today is that taking pictures $2\frac{1}{4}$ in. square on roll film, and they are designed to be used with a wide range of lenses from wide angle to telephoto. This type of camera is capable of producing excellent studies of birds.

Once again, a long focus lens is needed to bring up the image size, and once again the focal plane shutters are too noisy for most subjects. A silent or sectional shutter must be fitted between the lens and the mirror. With such an adaptation the focal plane shutter is kept in the fully open position while the supplementary shutter is being used.

Some can be fitted with plate backs for accurate focusing and this is an asset to the bird photographer using this type of camera from the confines of a hide. Modified in this way such a camera can be used for close quarter work, and a few bird photographers have even gone so far as to fit quite powerful telephotos up to 36 in.—often to single lens reflexes for taking birds on estuaries and sewage farms, and for similar "wait and see" subjects (See page 120). For such long distance work the focal plane shutter is used, and the camera and lens must be firmly supported.

The older type of single-lens reflex taking $3\frac{1}{2} \times 2\frac{1}{2}$ in. plates or larger is nowadays mostly replaced by the lighter and less cumbersome type just discussed. However a $3\frac{1}{2} \times 2\frac{1}{2}$ in. or quarter-plate reflex with a double extension bellows makes an excellent camera for birds. It can be used for close-ups at the nest, flight shots and long-distance work, in both colour and black-and-white. It has the advantage that the lens panel is readily detachable so that the usual 5 or 6 in. lens can be replaced by others of longer focal length.

When used close-up the noisy focal plane shutter is hopeless, but the fitting of a sectional or silent shutter behind the lens, probably on a special panel, is not a difficult matter.

As an alternative to the use of a separate shutter a lens may be fitted which is already set in a shutter. In this event all that is needed is to make an additional panel to accommodate this lens. When fitting such lenses it is important to see that the extension given by the bellows is adequate to permit focusing down to about four feet; some types with limited extensions may not permit this, which is why a double extension is desirable.

This kind of reflex has one main disadvantage—even the $3\frac{1}{2} \times 2\frac{1}{2}$ in. ones are rather heavy.

### Folding Plate Cameras

Cameras of the folding plate type, principally designed for $3\frac{1}{2} \times 2\frac{1}{2}$ in. or quarter-plate pictures, are equipped with lenses of too short a focal length for bird photography. On the other hand focusing is by ground-glass screen and many models have long bellows which allow a longer focus lens to be used. The adaptation of such cameras to take a silent shutter and a lens of $6\frac{1}{2}$–$8\frac{1}{2}$ in. focal length is not a difficult matter, though best tackled by a skilled mechanic. If a lens already fitted to a shutter is used however, the average photographer should be able to cope with the adaptation himself, since all that is usually needed is the removal of the existing shutter and lens assembly by slackening the locking collar and its replacement by the new combination. It may be necessary to enlarge the aperture in the camera front to admit the new lens. Such cameras are satisfactory for close-ups, particularly when used on a tripod, and since they are not much in demand nowadays they can be picked up quite cheaply—the more so if the lens and shutter fitted is to be scrapped anyway, for then the buyer's main consideration will be the condition of the body and the length of the bellows extension, and he can ignore a faulty shutter or a poor lens.

### Field Cameras

Field cameras taking quarter-plate pictures are popular with bird photographers for a number of very good reasons. It is a simple matter to adapt such cameras to take a silent shutter, and they are also readily fitted with lenses of various focal lengths simply by the provision of the additional lens panels. Furthermore, the ground glass screen method of focusing aids composition and is more convenient than the reflex system (or direct vision finders) when working within the confines of a hide. Last, but not least, the wide range of movements given by the swing back and rising front enables the photographer to cope with awkward branches, cliff walls and the like which would otherwise be out of focus and mar the results.

The general design of a field camera is very simple and a typical example is illustrated on page 21. It consists essentially of a long bellows held in a wooden framework which supports a detachable lens panel at the front and an adjustable back carrying the focusing screen.

In choosing a field camera special attention should be paid to the general condition of the framework, and in particular to the rigidity of the front which carries the lens panel. It is a good plan to purchase the body (including the dark slides) separate from the lens and shutter, as camera bodies can often be obtained for a few pounds. Half-plate cameras are usually plentiful, but quarter-plate size, which is the largest the bird-worker is likely to need, are not obtained so easily. However, an advertisement in the photographic press will usually produce offers.

If necessary a half-plate camera can be fitted with adaptors to enable quarter-plate or even $3\frac{1}{2} \times 2\frac{1}{2}$ in. materials to be used, but this means that one has to carry an unnecessarily bulky camera around when a smaller one would suffice. If possible the camera

---

CAMERAS AND SHUTTERS. The folding roll-film camera (1) and 35 mm. miniature with fixed lens (2) are suitable for large birds, record pictures of habitats and hides, and occasionally for flight pictures. Otherwise the camera should be capable of taking a long-focus lens, such as 9–13.5 cm. for a miniature (3, 4), $6\frac{1}{2}$ in. for a $2\frac{1}{4}$ in. sq. or $2\frac{1}{2} \times 3\frac{1}{2}$ in. reflex (5), or 8 in. for a $\frac{1}{4}$-plate field camera (6 and top right). A silent shutter (centre right) is also necessary and must be fitted behind the lens (4, 5). But for colour work an accurate shutter of the Prontor or Compur type is an advantage (bottom right), and the field camera is shown fitted with both types of shutter built into the front panel; note also its back focusing movement and deep lens hood.

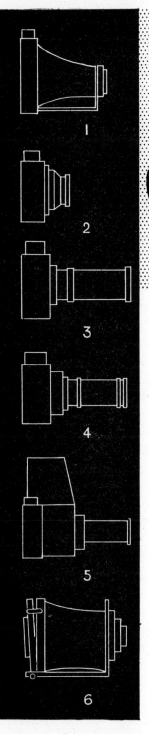

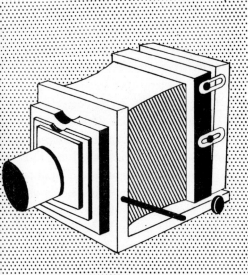

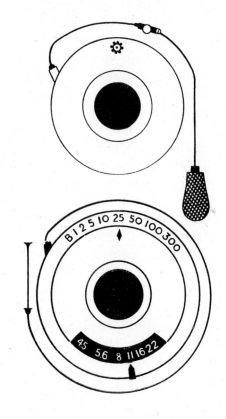

should have back focusing—that is, the back is moved towards or away from the front of the camera, whilst the lens remains stationary. This is a considerable advantage over front focusing since movement of the lens must be avoided in the presence of the subject.

Dark slides that are in correct register with the focusing screen are naturally essential. This should not be taken for granted but a newly acquired outfit should be carefully checked before being put into use. Double book-form slides as used with field cameras may not be light-tight when bought secondhand. It is often necessary to remove the draw-sheath and to renew the velvet light traps. The velvet around the camera back will also benefit by replacement, or at least by being steamed to raise the pile. The draw-sheaths should move easily in their grooves; if necessary they should be lubricated with a little soap, or perhaps rubbed down with fine glass-paper. Stiff slides are a menace in bird photography since they will creak noisily when used, and if much force has to be exerted in moving the draw-sheath or in inserting the slide in position, movement of the camera is probable and this in turn may alarm the sitter. Extra slides can often be purchased secondhand or they can be specially made.

The working of the rack and pinion should be firm and true. Slight wear which results in too free a movement of the camera back or front is undesirable since the slightest pressure, perhaps unnoticed (e.g. when removing or replacing the plate holder) may inadvertently alter the focus. If slackness is to be avoided so too is an excessively tight adjustment, since focusing may be accompanied by sundry creaks and groans from the camera—sounds likely to startle a nervous sitter. To correct either of these faults is not normally a difficult task.

Like other cameras the field camera has its limitations. It is essentially intended for use on a tripod, and is thus mainly used from the hide or for taking nests. This, however, covers the major part of the average bird photographer's activities. The beginner wishing to equip himself for this kind of work could not do better than to purchase a field camera; it will be found both effective and inexpensive.

In this review of the various camera types and their application to this special field of photography, it will be seen that some have certain advantages to offer over others. Thus those who do a lot of this sort of camera work, and can afford them, have several cameras each of which is used according to the requirements of the moment. The writer has two quarter-plate field cameras (one for colour and one for black and white); a $3\frac{1}{2} \times 2\frac{1}{2}$ in. reflex which will take a long focus lens and a silent shutter, and which is used for long distance work and for a certain number of flight shots; a coupled-rangefinder rollfilm camera for general record photography; and a 35 mm. camera for making colour transparencies for projection.

## The Lens

In bird photography, as in all camera work where accurate portrayal of fact is aimed at, it is desirable to show the finest detail, and the crispness of the feather rendering of a bird portrait depends ultimately on the quality and resolution of the lens. For reasons already explained it is often impossible to bring the camera as near to the subject as could be done were it an inanimate object of the same size, and a lens of reasonably long focal length is generally used; one of $8-8\frac{1}{4}$ in. focal length is very popular with bird photographers using field cameras. For the miniature a 7.5–9 cm. lens will be found satisfactory. Such lenses provide images of a suitable size at practicable working distances without losing too much depth of field. For example, at a distance of 7 ft. from a lapwing sitting sideways to the camera, an image of the bird measuring a little over $1\frac{1}{4}$ in. is given when an $8\frac{1}{4}$ in. lens is used. This is a very convenient image size for a quarter-plate negative as it allows ample room to include plenty of surroundings, and yet shows the bird large enough to bring out all the fine plumage detail.

If the $8-8\frac{1}{4}$ in. lens is the most widely used among British bird photographers, many also employ lenses of shorter focal length with success, though few apart from miniaturists seem to find anything less than 6 in. of much practical value. The author has found a 6½ in. (16.5 cm.) lens very convenient, particularly in conjunction with 3½ × 2½ in. material.

It should be noted that although good quality lenses are desirable, these need not be of wide aperture. An f4.5 lens gives a brighter image for focusing, but a good lens of f6.3 or smaller will be found adequate for most purposes.

The lens should be carefully checked for resolution; there is often quite a marked variation in this respect between supposedly identical lenses by the same manufacturer. Secondhand lenses if in sound condition are often fully satisfactory, and a first-rate f6.3 anastigmat in Compur shutter can be bought secondhand for five pounds. Bloomed lenses are an improvement on those not so treated and should be purchased if funds permit.

When making a start at bird photography it is advisable to use only one lens at first. Gradually, as the learner acquires skill in his pursuit, he will appreciate the limitations of working with a single lens and may acquire others to suit his special needs and interests. Thus, if he is going to attempt the photography of wildfowl on a lake in winter, the need for a telephoto or long focus lens to bring his elusive subjects into range will soon be apparent; likewise if he tries to portray swallows nesting in a shed where space is limited he may need one of shorter focal length to overcome his difficulties.

A lens hood, as deep as possible, is a necessity; it should be painted green on the outside. The type which is threaded to screw on to the front lens component is perhaps ideal, for the hood cannot drop off at the wrong moment as sometimes happens with those that are merely slipped on to the lens barrel.

### The Shutter

Although it is remarkable how accustomed some birds will become to unusual and even irregular noises, many will never quite overcome their uneasiness at the sound of even the quietest shutter. The more silent the shutter the more likely is the bird photographer to succeed in his efforts in showing his subjects at their ease.

Before the last war a simple sectional shutter made in Germany, the Luc, was widely used in this country for nature photography. Pre-war Luc shutters are still in use, but British and imported ones of similar design, like the Day, are now readily available. These shutters have three leaves which open quietly when the release is pressed and then close quickly with a slight click as the blades fall together. Thus, if the subject does start at the sound, this happens after the exposure has been made and movement is not apparent on the negative.

With this shutter the length of the exposure is governed by the speed at which the release plunger is pressed. It is possible, therefore, without altering the setting to get any exposure from very slow (say $\frac{1}{2}$ sec.) to about 1/40 sec., which is the maximum speed. Should the lighting conditions be variable, as when there is intermittent cloud, correctly exposed negatives may be obtained by adjusting the pressure and the resulting exposure accordingly.

Such "silent" shutters have three settings: an "Instantaneous" one, where the duration of the exposure is controlled by the pressure as already described; a "Brief" setting, where pressure on the release opens the leaves for as long as the pressure is maintained—at this setting the shutter can be used to give exposures of about $\frac{1}{2}$ second longer and the closure of the blades is almost inaudible; and a third setting for opening the shutter fully for focusing. A modern shutter of this type is illustrated on page 21.

Nowadays silent shutters are available with internal synchronization for flash and with accurate timing devices for colour work, and they come in a variety of sizes and patterns.

The original Luc was intended to be used in front of the lens, and three screws were provided to fasten it to the barrel of the lens mount. Such an arrangement is unsuitable for bird work. The movement of the shutter blades would be visible from in front, and the sudden revelation of the eye-like lens beneath would hardly increase the bird's confidence in the hide and its contents. For bird work a silent shutter must be mounted behind the lens; it is set in a housing attached to the front of the camera and designed so that a lens panel or panels can be fitted in front as desired. The adaptation of a field camera in this way and the making of the necessary housing for the shutter is easily undertaken by anyone handy with tools. Thin seasoned wood will be required—old whole-plate bookform slides are an ideal source; even the proverbial cigar box may prove useful here. Alternatively, the lens and shutter may be adapted to fit on to each other, the work being undertaken by firms handling camera repairs or possibly by the suppliers of the shutter.

Shutters such as the Compound, Compur and Prontor make more noise than those of the Luc pattern and suffer from the disadvantage that, except on "Brief", many of them must be reset after each exposure. This is a disadvantage not only because of the time lag between exposures, but also because of the additional "click" of the mechanism as the shutter is cocked. Furthermore, should the light change during the session, and it frequently does, the alteration of both shutter setting and iris diaphragm is not particularly easy, due to the restricted space within which the photographer is working. On the other hand such shutters, if correctly adjusted and maintained, enable consistent exposures to be given and they are therefore particularly suitable for colour work where the need for really accurate exposures makes the use of some silent types rather difficult. On "Brief" the Compur and Prontor are practically noiseless and may be used for long exposures with success.

It is possible to design the panels of the field camera so that a lens fitted in a Compur or Prontor shutter can be fixed in front of the silent one. Thus either may be used with the same lens as called for by the needs of the moment, the silent one being left open when the Compur is in use, and *vice versa.*

Post-war cable releases have not been notable for their reliability. The uncovered types soon develop kinks, and once the inner cable ceases to run smoothly inside the casing vibrations are easily set up and camera shake may result—with all its attendant troubles. Cloth-covered releases are better but are still unable to withstand much hard wear. An 18 in. release is a useful size; 36 in. ones are made and these are handy when the camera is placed rather high in relation to one's sitting position, since the long release enables the shutter to be controlled without having to hold the hand in a tiring posture whilst awaiting an opportunity for an exposure. On the other hand, in bird photography it is essential to anticipate the moment at which the subject will be stationary, and the shorter the time lag between the brain's decision that the shutter should be opened and the actual exposure, the greater the likelihood of a successful picture resulting. Control of the timing is easier with short cable releases since there is inevitably a greater play with a long release than with a short one. Long releases are also more likely to become strained than are shorter ones. Some silent type shutters are operated by pneumatic releases; these are quite vibration free and are greatly to be recommended. With miniature cameras a cable release should be used in preference to the body release; this is more comfortable and lessens the risk of camera shake.

## The Tripod

It cannot be over-emphasized that the tripod should be strong and rigid. On no account should rigidity be sacrificed for lightness; a dithering tripod is worse than useless. If funds allow it is a good plan to have two tripods. One extending to about 3 ft. will serve for use in situations where the camera is to be placed low down, such as when working ground-nesting birds. A larger one with an extension sufficient to raise the camera to 5 or 6 ft. can then be employed for higher situations. Wooden models with folding or sliding legs are often quite satisfactory, although there may be a tendency for the wood to swell when wet and the legs not slide up properly until they have been dried out. The slides must be kept free of dirt or mud or they will become clogged and useless.

A tilting top is a "must" for the bird worker since it is so often necessary to tilt the camera without moving the tripod legs. Ball and socket devices are rarely strong enough, and a simple arrangement made of two leaves of wood hinged together, and held at the required angle by metal struts and wing nuts, is recommended. Such a tilt-top is easily made or can be bought quite cheaply. A typical pattern is shown on page 29. The miniaturist will probably find a good cine pan-and-tilt head ideal.

## The Exposure Meter

The bird photographer has to work in so many different situations and under such variable lighting conditions that the judgement of exposures is often difficult. From the confines of a hide it is very easy to over-estimate the amount of light falling upon the subject, and the value of a reliable photoelectric meter as an insurance against wasted film is considerable. It is essential when working in colour.

## Materials

Indifferent lighting conditions will compel the use of fast pan. materials, and this can be done with the minimum loss of quality if a fine grain developer is employed. Plates are very convenient since at the end of a session a few may be developed as a trial and the processing of the main batch conducted accordingly. Cut films may be used in the same manner of course; they seem to be superseding plates and have the advantage of lightness—and they do not break if dropped on to the darkroom floor.

Many workers using the larger cameras rely solely on plates or cut film and regard roll-films as too troublesome to be worthwhile, not because of intrinsic defect in the film but because of the difficulty of obtaining a roll holder (necessary for using roll-film in a stand camera) which does not give rise to scratches. But once a reliable holder has been found it can be a most useful tool. Roll-films have not only the advantage of lightness and cheapness, but with a little practice they can be wound from one exposure to the next by counting the turns required instead of using the red window. More turns are needed at the beginning of the roll than towards the end. In this way a series of pictures may be made in

---

TRIPOD AND FITTINGS. The tripod must be both strong and rigid and able to withstand rough usage (bottom right). For ground nests it requires to extend to about 3 ft. and for higher situations to about 5 or 6 ft. A tilting top is essential, and the type consisting of two hinged wooden plattens with side struts (bottom left) is both efficient and easy to make. A board to carry two cameras, one for black-and-white pictures and one for colour, is a useful accessory (left centre). The cameras are fitted to separate tilting tops bolted to each end of the board; the complete arrangement is shown at the top of the page.

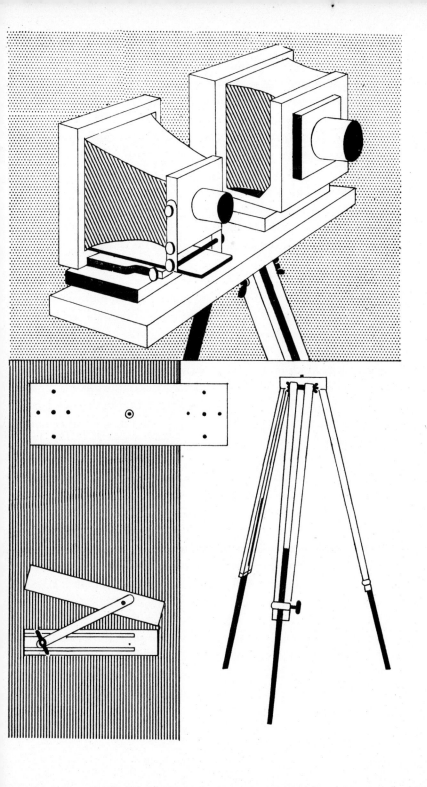

quite rapid succession without the finger being taken off the release plunger, and this is an obvious asset. Furthermore, a second holder loaded with colour film enables the camera to be used for both black-and-white and colour photography. The author invariably carries a loaded roll holder and spare films which are used to supplement plates; when the latter are exhausted the roll holder is brought into use—for $3\frac{1}{4} \times 2\frac{1}{4}$ in. pictures, of course. The plate holders can then be reloaded if necessary, using a changing bag. If a roll holder is employed scrupulous cleanliness is essential and the carrier and the inside of the body should be thoroughly dusted out every time the film is changed.

### Colour Requirements

Birds are colourful creatures, colourful both in plumage and in personality; and even though many magnificent species inhabit the tropics, the birds of the northern hemisphere include many of brilliant plumage—the kingfisher, for instance. And there are many other kinds no less attractive for their more restrained hues. In a setting of green leaves the delicate tones of the turtle dove are a fine sight; the buffs and browns of the sitting woodcock blend wonderfully into the leaf-strewn background despite the richness of the colouring; green woodpeckers with gallant red moustachios are gaudy creatures crying out for the colour camera; even the familiar and gluttonous starling is a joy to behold as it sits spluttering in exuberant song with the spring sunlight dancing off its feathers in a sheen of purple and green.

People have tried for years to photograph birds in colour, but until the appearance of colour film in a form that enabled the use of reasonably short exposures, this was a very difficult task.

The photographer is well provided for today. There is a wide range of colour films, both the reversal type giving transparencies direct, and the negative type for making colour prints. All sizes are available—35 mm., roll films and sheet films—and most of them can be processed by the user should he wish to do so. The speed of colour films, too, is subject to constant improvement. Colour film however, is expensive and processing costs more and is more elaborate than with black-and-white material; the high cost partly accounts for the popularity of the smaller sizes with the amateur worker.

Although working with 35 mm. film allows many more pictures to be taken for the same outlay, the author's preference is to use $3\frac{1}{4} \times 2\frac{1}{4}$ roll film and quarter-plate flat film and to take correspondingly fewer pictures. For those who do not already possess a miniature, the bigger sizes should commend themselves since sheet film is easily loaded into the standard plate holders, while if you use roll film it can be masked down to give smaller pictures—twelve $2\frac{1}{4} \times 2\frac{1}{4}$ in. or sixteen $2\frac{1}{4} \times 1\frac{5}{8}$ in.—in place of the eight $3\frac{1}{4} \times 2\frac{1}{4}$ in. ones. Those who already own a miniature camera will find it of use on occasions when the birds are tame and unlikely to be frightened by the shutter, and especially if a longer focus lens can be fitted to increase the image size so that it is unnecessary to get too close to the sitter. Black-and-white copy negatives can be made from transparencies on slow panchromatic emulsions and ordinary prints made from them without much loss of detail and quality. Similarly separation negatives may be made for the production of colour prints by Trichrome Carbro, Dye Transfer, Duxochrome and allied processes. The negative type of film is of course designed to produce colour prints direct, and ordinary black-and-white prints can be made from the negatives, although there is some distortion in the final rendering of the colours in the subject.

Bird photography in colour calls for no drastic change in technique from black-and-white, but on account of the slowness of the material compared with a fast panchromatic emulsion, and its expense, your first subjects should be ones that are not too active. A robin would be very suitable. The average worker can no longer afford to take many risks, and he is therefore forced to use wider apertures not only on account of the slowness of the material, but also to speed up his exposures and lessen the risk of wastage due to movement. With such apertures focusing must be done very carefully, and the use of stops on the camera baseboard as described on page 67 is often helpful.

Colour films have only a slight latitude and exposure must be just right if acceptable results are to be obtained. A reliable exposure meter of the photo-electric type is essential to measure the light reflected by the nest and its surroundings. Nor are the films capable of handling high contrasts, and to ensure that this condition is complied with several readings on different parts of the subject must be made. With birds whose plumage is not neutral in tone—with a gull or a rook for instance—some sort of matt card may be needed to represent the bird. For a rook a black card and for a gull a white or cream one would be used from which to take a reading. If in doubt, it is best to expose for the bird and let the surroundings take care of themselves, for the bird is the important feature and if it is shown in its true colouring some inaccuracy in the surroundings is permissible. As the light is liable to fluctuate it is important that readings taken on the nest be checked against the reflection from the ground at the back of the hide, as described on page 67. In this way any alterations in the light value can be assessed and the stop altered accordingly.

There is no point in establishing the correct exposure if the shutter used is unreliable. The old type Luc shutters do not enable accurate exposures to be given for few people can judge the amount of pressure necessary for precise control. A speeded sectional shutter is needed, and this should be checked from time to time (perhaps every two years) by a reliable firm to see that the speeds given are really accurate and consistent. There is also at least one shutter of the Luc type on the market which is operated by a pneumatic release and which incorporates an inexpensive timing device giving exposures of 1/25, 1/5, ½, 1 and 2 secs. with sufficient reliability for colour photography.

If the colour film requires a correction filter, these are of thin gelatin and may be conveniently fixed between the lens components where they are protected from dust and finger-marks. Alternatively they may be mounted between optical flats and used in a filter holder fitted to the lens. If the same lens is used for monochrome and colour then the filter holder will be more convenient, since it can be easily removed. If you can keep one lens only for colour, then any filter needed can be placed permanently inside the lens. The removal of a filter is not easy once you are inside the hide, for if the bird is sitting it will not regard your hand, slipping out to detach the filter mount, as a pleasant surprise, though this may be possible while the birds are away feeding. Sometimes it may be more convenient to fit the filter at the back of the lens so that it can be taken off when required from the rear through the bellows; but in this case if the filter is mounted between glass you must focus the camera with the filter in position.

I like to use two cameras side by side, one of which is reserved for colour and has any filter necessary incorporated in the lens system. This camera, together with a second one for monochrome pictures, is mounted on a drilled and bushed board so that both may be fixed to the one tripod. The cameras each have their own tilt top so that they may be positioned independently. The board must be long enough for the draw sheaths of the left-hand camera to be pulled out without coming into contact with the right-hand one.

When making a start in the colour photography of birds it is an excellent plan to keep a careful record of the first dozen exposures. Such notes should include the meter readings of high-light and shadow areas, the actual exposure given, the batch number of the film and the type of filter used. By checking finished transparencies against these details you will be able to ensure the best results on subsequent occasions.

Colour film has a shorter life than monochrome so that only sufficient for foreseen needs should be purchased at a time; out—of-date film often shows incorrect colour balance.

Sea-birds are very suitable subjects for the colour camera as the light is generally very good and short exposures may be possible. In such places you will often need a haze filter to cut down the ultra violet light which is always above normal near the sea; ultra violet registers as blue on the film. A similar filter may be necessary when working beside a large expanse of water, particularly if there are blue skies overhead.

## The Hide

A most important item in the bird photographer's kit is the hide. This is a device whereby the watcher or photographer can be concealed within working distance of his subject. Sometimes local materials are used in its construction, such as reeds, stones or turf, but a made-up hide of canvas or similar fabric will be found essential.

A simple form is shown diagrammatically on page 35. It consists of a box-shaped cover made from thick cotton sheeting, sacking or hessian (dyed or sprayed with paint in a green or brownish shade) sewn completely around at the top and down three sides— one side being left unstitched. This unstitched side allows access to the hide when it is erected on the framework which holds it in position.

A simple, cheap, and durable hide frame may be made from four pieces of heavy gauge ⅝ in. welded electrical conduit each about 5 to 5½ ft. long. One end of each piece is flattened with a hammer and shaped to a point which is easily forced into the ground. Four pieces of stout galvanized wire (8 to 10 gauge is satisfactory, and about 3 ft. 6 in. long) are then required, and the last three inches of the ends bent down at right-angles. These are inserted into the open ends of the tops of the conduit when the latter are driven into the ground about 3 ft. apart.

The covering is made to fit the size of the hide and draped over the framework; it is drawn tight and the open sides fastened with strong safety pins. Guy ropes from each corner of the top are desirable as they contribute greatly to the stability of the structure,

HIDES. A portable hide is a necessary part of the bird photographer's equipment. The frame may consist of four uprights of electrical conduit with galvanized wire connecting pieces at the top (2). The ends of the uprights are flattened and pointed (4) so they can be pushed into the ground. It is a useful refinement if the uprights are adjustable for height (3); the top section (A) slides into a bottom section of larger diameter (C) and is secured by a Jubilee clip (B). A hessian or canvas cover is slipped over the frame, and the completed side secured by guy lines (5). Comdr. A. W. P. Robertson's "mobile" hide (see page 98) has a wooden base frame (I); the conduit uprights push on to pegs at the corners, and the frame folds for carrying and is provided with holes for staking down.

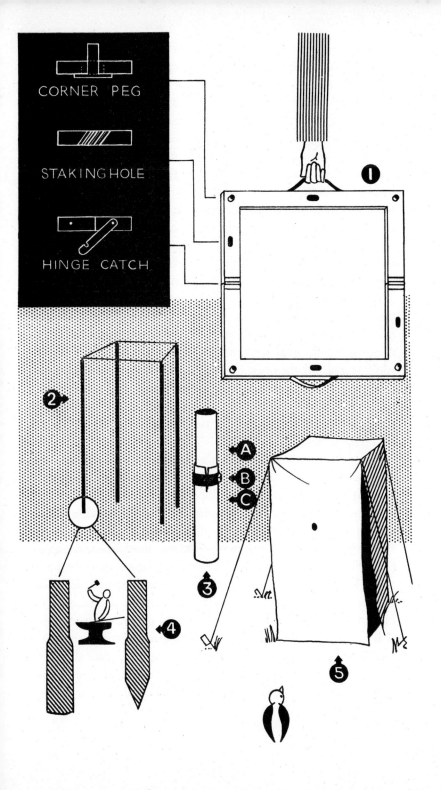

CORNER PEG

STAKING HOLE

HINGE CATCH

especially in windy weather and in exposed situations. Normal tent cord runners and pegs are used.

The kind of fabric from which the covering is made is important; colour matters less than opacity. Birds have very good eyesight and when the sun is shining on a hide of thin material they will easily detect the silhouette of anyone inside. Industrial sheeting of a heavy grade, dyed brown or green—the more patchy the dyeing the better—is very satisfactory though rather expensive. Hessian sold in yard-wide lengths may also be used, but is not completely impervious to light, and extra pieces of material may have to be pinned up at the back or on the sunny side when the hide is in use. Hessian shrinks a lot when wet, which is sometimes rather a nuisance, but it is comparatively cheap.

Beware of rubberized fabrics. Hides made from these can be veritable purgatories in hot weather since they allow so little circulation of air. And when rain falls on a rubber roof the drumming of the drops is sometimes so great that the birds may be badly scared, for the noise is much louder than the normal patter of rain on foliage to which they are accustomed. If a waterproof roof is desired the rubberized material should be fitted below a cotton or hessian roof so that the rain cannot fall directly on to the proofed material.

A simple hide made of conduit as described above will be found adequate for a very large number of situations and can often be used on ground having a slight slope, since by driving some of the uprights in further than the others the top may be kept horizontal. But on steeper hillsides and in similar situations it becomes necessary to have short uprights on one side. For this purpose telescopic or adjustable uprights are best. These can be made in a number of ways, but one of the simplest and best is to construct each from two pieces of conduit, each say 3 ft. in length, one piece being of $\frac{1}{2}$ in. size and the other $\frac{5}{8}$ in. so that the narrower piece, which will form the upper half of the upright, can slide inside the lower one. The idea is illustrated on page 35. The $\frac{5}{8}$ in. piece should be of the type known as welded or seamed conduit, and one end of this should be squeezed in to form a wedged-shaped point, or a metal point can be fitted. At the other end a downward cut is made with a hacksaw for about an inch so that the tube can be pressed in to grip the $\frac{1}{2}$ in. conduit sliding up and down inside. To the top of the wider piece, at the point where the cuts have been made, a small hose clip is fitted (preferably welded on) and this, when tightened, clamps the inner tube in position. A coin or small screwdriver is used for adjusting the clip.

Hides made from conduit in this manner are not expensive and they have the advantage of packing into quite a small space; the metal itself is not very heavy. Metal poles have a few disadvantages, more particularly that it is not easy to fix anything to them. When wooden uprights are used it is easy and convenient to have one or two nails or hooks on the inside of the hide on which to hang a jacket or camera cases; and things such as flash reflectors and lights are more easily fastened to wood than to iron. Despite this, conduit is probably the best and simplest material to employ.

When a hide is used at ground level a folding seat is desirable. This should be strong, for it will often have to be used on irregular surfaces where there will be a fair amount of strain on the framework, and it should be of the type in which the cross-struts on the legs are set high enough up for the ends of the legs to sink slightly into the ground if need be. This gives a firmer seat when working on moist, peaty and soft ground generally.

# Birds and their Nests

THE VAST MAJORITY of bird photographs, even today, are taken at or in the vicinity of nests and this chapter deals with how to go about the photography of the common birds of garden and wood (to which species the beginner is urged to confine his first attempts) which nest either on the ground or at not more than shoulder height in trees, bushes or undergrowth.

"Bird-at-the-nest" photography is popular not only because breeding behaviour is of great intrinsic interest, and because both sexes may attend the young, but because the cameraman's basic problem of how to get near enough to his subject is solved by the bird's attraction to its nest, provided only that he can overcome the natural shyness of such a quarry. Few birds, however strongly attached to their eggs or young, will remain while you walk up to the nest camera in hand; concealment is essential and is provided by the hide, which will be accepted by the birds as part of the landscape if it is properly presented to them, despite its obvious artificiality to the human eye.

Do not be deluded by the occasional photographs you may see of apparently tame birds photographed without a hide, such as willow warblers perching on human fingers. Some birds may indeed pluck up sufficient courage to feed their chicks in full view of the unconcealed observer, but this imposes an unwarrantable strain on the parents who already have all their work cut out to rear their brood. Such methods are very liable to lead to the young being deserted, with consequent loss of life, and are greatly to be deprecated.

38

## Choice of Subjects

The beginner is recommended to choose as his first subjects those birds which are usually tolerant towards human beings and therefore not difficult to photograph. Robins, chaffinches, starlings and titmice are kinds often found in gardens and woods which are seldom camera shy. On pages 172–195 is given a list of other common species with notes on their nesting sites, reactions to the camera, and the distances at which the latter should be placed in order to get images of satisfactory sizes on plate and film. Note however, that birds, like you or me, are of varying temperaments and two individuals of the same species may be quite different in their reactions to the hide; one may be as timid as most members of its kind are confiding.

In my opinion it is essential for the novice to avoid trying to do too much in one brief nesting season. He should be content to get practice in the skills which must be mastered before good work can be produced without harming his subjects. Many attractive opportunities for pictures may occur in the course of a spring and summer, but the beginner should limit his activities according to the time which is available and not hurry from one nest to another before the lessons of the first have been taken to heart.

## Where to Work

You must have somewhere to work. Public parks and gardens are quite unsuitable, for the bird photographer must have privacy so that he may site his hides without attracting the attention of passers-by. Much can be done in large gardens where freedom from interference is assured, but the range of species in such environments is limited and access to some wooded estate or to open moors is desirable. The more strictly the latter is keepered the more the photographer benefits, and provided he can gain the confidence of the landowner and his servants by his integrity and care, particularly as regards game birds, he will find them all very helpful and sympathetic to his aims. And, of course, a batch of prints at the end of the season is the least one can do in return.

## Nest Finding

First find your bird and its nest. Sometimes others will find them for you—gamekeepers may point them out, for instance—but by and large the photographer must be his own field worker. He must be prepared to spend a good deal of time in the preliminaries before any photographs can be taken.

Nest hunting can be tiring, and in some types of country, exhausting. Often it is easy; much depends on the terrain, on your experience and for what you are searching. The beginner, looking only for any suitable subject, will not encounter much difficulty, although he may find that some days bring few successes whilst on others he stumbles on interesting finds at every turn.

There are two ways of locating nests—either by physical searching of likely places, or by watching the adult birds until their actions reveal their secrets. The latter method is often effective when you can watch an area through binoculars either without the birds being aware of your presence, or from a distance such that despite their being able to see you they are not sufficiently scared to visit the nest. This method is very useful with small birds feeding young still in the nest, since at such times their visits are frequent and the old birds seldom very timid. The point at which they disappear with food in their beaks is noted (if necessary in relation to some adjacent prominent object) and you can then walk up, and by inspecting the bushes or foliage, can normally find the nest without much further trouble.

In difficult situations the birds' movements may be watched from two different angles, thus obtaining a very clear indication of the precise location of the nest. The more you know about the birds' habits, about the size, placing and construction of the nest, the easier discovery will be. This wait-and-see procedure is most effective with small birds like warblers, finches, titmice and so on, since these readily perch on branches and stalks where they can be be easily picked out as they move to and fro. It is not feasible with birds like duck, pipits, partridges and other kinds which build in deep vegetation and approach beneath thick cover, since this conceals their movements. Nor is it of much help with birds of broad horizons, like lapwings and curlews, for these will seldom return to their eggs while being watched, even if from a distance, though they will often do so if you are sitting in a car or truck.

Lapwings are particularly cunning birds, and their behaviour is typical of that of most members of the plover family in whatever part of the world you may observe them. Nesting right out in the open on pasture or arable land they are able to spot the intruder from afar and walk off their eggs when you are still hundreds of yards away. They peck about nonchalantly as if feeding and at the same time edge further and further away from their nests. By the time you get near enough to cause them to fly up they are many yards from the eggs and you may search in vain for their secret.

Such guile is best countered by greater guile. It is easy to tell from the birds' deceitful attitudes, from their excited aerial flights and anxious calls, whether they have a nest in a particular field. It is then necessary to examine the lie of the land to see if it is possible to get to the edge of the field without being seen by the birds. Perhaps there may be a ditch, a bank or a hedge running along one side by which an approach can be made. If such a concealed route does exist it is used on a subsequent visit, and when right at the edge of the field, still concealed and ready to note the point at which the bird arises, you jump suddenly into view. The nesting bird will either fly straight off the eggs or will run away from them. In either event, without looking to right or left, you walk forward to the point from which the bird arose. If the eggs are not immediately apparent, place something on the ground (the binoculars will do) and a little further searching nearby should reveal them. I have often used this method both at home and abroad when seeking the nests of birds which lay in the open. The method may be appropriate to any situation where a concealed approach is possible along a belt of trees, a sunken road or fold in the ground, or through a wood adjoining the open nesting area and from the shelter of which a sudden emergence can be made. If two people employ the dodge simultaneously from different directions, their paths should intersect at the nest.

41

Many nests may be found by searching shrubberies or other likely cover. This is most effective in early spring before the bushes are clothed with leaves, and when you know the area and the birds that have formerly bred there it is surprising how favoured a certain spot will be year after year. When inspecting bushes and hedgerows it is best to bend down and peer upwards so that any nests are silhouetted against the sky.

On searching among rank and low herbage many species such as whitethroats, warblers, duck and so on may be flushed from their nests which they do not leave until the very last moment. A greater area may be covered by using a long twig which is drawn along the foliage as you work through it.

When a bird is suspected of breeding in a given area and other methods have failed to locate its precise whereabouts, systematic searching may be the answer, the whole area being carefully quartered to a definite plan. A nest discovered in deep vegetation or other situations where there are no clear guides to its position, should be marked to enable the spot to be found readily on a later occasion. A stick placed in the ground a few yards away often serves the purpose; it should be perfectly clear to yourself but not sufficiently obvious to attract anyone else's attention.

*Nests and Eggs*

The nests and eggs of birds building within five feet of the ground are generally easily photographed. Others may be difficult to take because of their awkward placing. A magpie's nest in a tall thorn hedge would be a tough proposition, and for much the same reason we seldom see pictures of the contents of rooks' nests high in the trees, nor of the eggs of hole-nesting kinds like the stock dove.

---

PHOTOGRAPHING NESTS. In trees the tripod may be lashed to branches (1) or the camera fixed to a branch by means of a bracket of some kind (2). Useful dodges for fairly high nests are to lash extension pieces to the tripod legs (3), or use two ladders tied at the top (4). A short tripod may be an asset for nests on the ground (5), but one of normal height is suitable for nests in bushes and vegetation (6). Nests at the waterside may be rather inaccessible and hemmed in by reeds and vegetation; but favourably sited nests present few problems (7).

From a hide the nest is viewed at a rather shallow angle for the camera is placed to show the birds properly; but when taking photographs of the eggs a much higher viewpoint is required. The usual procedure is to tilt the camera at about 75 degrees to the horizontal so that all the eggs are visible, and to give a time exposure with the lens stopped fully down. In a picture of this kind everything should be in focus. A tilting top is essential to bring the camera to bear at the required angle. Focusing should not be done casually just because it is intended to close down to $f32$ or more; accuracy is still needed and attention should also be paid to the composition of the picture. Minor trimmings of the surroundings are generally needed.

With time exposures there is some risk of camera shake. An old dodge is to make the exposure by holding a card (which does not touch any part of the camera) a note-book or a draw sheath in front of the lens, to open the shutter, and after a moment's pause, to remove the card for the necessary number of seconds before re-covering the lens and closing the shutter. Any vibration taking place when the shutter is opened is nullified with this method. The idea will not work when there is a wind to move the vegetation or to vibrate the camera. It is then best to give a series of instantaneous exposures during moments when the foliage is at rest. For example, the meter may indicate an exposure of 1 sec. at $f32$. This could be given in the form of five 1/5 sec. exposures slipped in during momentary lulls.

A point to remember when working with colour film is that time exposures may require additional filters to maintain proper colour balance; where this is necessary appropriate instructions are usually enclosed with the film.

Awkwardly placed nests may call for a variety of devices to bring the camera to bear at a convenient angle. In the case of the magpie's nest it might be necessary to set up a scaffold to over-look it or to use a pair of ladders lashed together to form a large pair of steps. Tree-top nests also involve a good deal of work. Sometimes you can lash a tripod to the branches and fasten the camera on in the usual way. If so, well and good, but as often as not the idea is impracticable. But the camera must be fixed some-how, for pictures taken in the hand when you are perched pre-cariously in the tree tops invariably suffer from camera shake.

An idea I have used with success is to screw a wooden bracket to a branch or trunk above the nest and at a suitable distance from it. This bracket is drilled to admit a tripod screw at one end and the other is nailed or screwed to the branch or tree trunk. The tilt top is then fitted on the free end so that the camera can be focused and positioned correctly. Various universal clamps are available on the market and they could be used for the same purpose.

Nests and eggs are often objects of beauty in their own right and often justify the use of colour, the more so since there is little risk of wastage if exposure is correctly determined. Even the commonest of species can provide the makings of a beautiful picture.

### Young Birds

Until recently pictures of callow nestlings perched side by side on some flower-decked branch were commonplace in the spring-time issues of illustrated magazines. Fashions change—in this in-stance for the better—and although an incipient rash of such pic-tures crops up from time to time, it seems to be more widely appreciated that the attitudes shown are unnatural and the photo-graphs merely records of ignorance.

Most bird photographers have been guilty of similar misde-meanours, at least during their early days, but the practice is a bad one for several reasons. When young birds are almost ready to fledge the slightest interference sends them scurrying prematurely from the nest in all directions. The family is broken up and many of the chicks perish; the mortality rate if they are undisturbed is high enough during their first few days out of the nest without their having to suffer additional losses at the hands of inconsider-ate photographers. The would-be photographer of nestlings soon finds that he must choose those not yet fully grown as they prove less flighty and more amenable to handling. They may be induced to perch after a fashion, but their legs are weak, some can hardly grasp the branch at all, others slump down on their haunches, and instead of looking lively and attractive, they look as miserable as fish out of water. The experienced bird worker will have nothing to do with this sort of thing.

If pictures of nestlings are needed to complete a series they should be taken *in situ* during the youngsters' last days in the nest; just occasionally you may come across a well feathered fledgeling bold enough to allow a close approach as it stands erect and natural on a branch, and then a hand-held camera may be very useful to take it before it decides to move. Electronic flash enables interesting pictures to be made of the youngsters' activities in their nurseries—their behaviour when preening, when exercising their wings and so on, and the begging attitudes of young nidicolous species may make interesting and amusing photographs.

### Selecting a Nest for Hide Photography

Not each and every nest will be suitable for photography; with the common birds there is no point in trying to work the first nest that is found. It is better to wait until several sites are available and then to select those most suitable bearing in mind the points below:—

1. Where the hide can be placed.
2. The position of the nest and hide in relation to the sun.
3. The amount of "gardening" that will be required.
4. The possibility of human interference.
5. The background.

Let us consider these factors one by one.

1. *Placing the hide.* At many nests you will have only a limited choice of positions in which the hide can be set up to bring the camera to the correct height and taking distance. For example, if the nest is in a large bramble bush, the hide will have to be placed on the side of the bush at which the nest is situated; likewise in woods and other places the room for manœuvre may be limited. In contrast, with nests in the open, like those of the plovers, the hide may be pitched in any required position. Some ground nesting birds like skylarks and pipits conceal their homes in clumps of

grass, and there is usually only one suitable position from which a good view is possible.

2. *The lighting* of the site is obviously important. The sun is due south at noon (G.M.T.) in the northern hemisphere, which means that if the hide is placed south of the nest the sun will shine from the right in the morning and from the left in the afternoon. South of the equator, of course, the reverse applies. Strong sunlight is often prejudicial to good bird photography because of the harsh contrasts it creates, but the sun's position must, nevertheless, be considered, as well as the probable time of the day when you expect to be able to do the photography. A slightly veiled sun is ideal for bird work. Note that when the sun is shining it may throw the shadow of the hide across the nest and thereby complicate matters. In circumstances where it is impossible to site the hiding tent so that the sun will be to one flank or to the rear, then you have to work either against the light or solely when the sun is clouded over. It may be better not to try working such a nest.

3. By *"gardening"* is meant the removal of grasses, branches and other vegetation from the sides and front of the nest when this is needed to give the camera an unimpeded view. This opening up can only be done with care since it means directly interfering with the nest's immediate surroundings, and your first consideration must be for the safety and well-being of the birds themselves. Thus the experienced worker leaves untouched those nests which are placed in deep cover where extensive trimming would be required; he prefers to wait until a more suitable site is discovered. Frequently an otherwise excellent nest must be turned down because some twig or branch supporting the nest obstructs the view.

It will be clear from all this that the amount and type of trimming needed before a nest can be photographed is an important factor which must be considered when weighing its possibilities. Furthermore, everything else being equal, the time taken to get the hide in position and ready for the camera will be greater at a nest needing a lot of gardening, since this opening up can only be done by stages and this might add several days to the preparatory period.

4. *Human interference.* It should be the rule that no attempt is

made to photograph nests in spots where the setting up of the hide is likely to attract the attention of other people. Despite camouflage, it is often impossible to conceal a hide sufficiently to deceive a human eye, and inquisitive people, children and youths, even if not intending to do any harm, may unwittingly destroy nests or cause the parent birds to desert. In woods and in private grounds the danger is far less and hides are fairly easy to conceal in such places. On open fields they are best sited where they are overlooked by some farm or cottage whose owners will keep a watchful eye on any intruders.

In lush vegetation tracks soon appear if the same route is used on successive visits to a nest; such revealing tracks should be avoided by varying the route on each occasion. Many otherwise excellent sites must be passed over because of the danger of human interference, but it is not only people that are inquisitive—beware of cattle. Hides set up in places to which cattle have access are doomed from the start. The herd is soon on the spot to ascertain the nature of the erection; they try to use it as a rubbing post. In no time at all both nest and hide are in ruins. A post and barbed-wire enclosure fencing in both nest and hide is the best way out, if special considerations warrant the working of nests in such places.

5. *Background.* In weighing up whether a nest fits the bird photographer's bill, the nature of the background must be taken into consideration. Some sites are ruled out at once on this score and ugly obtrusive backgrounds can easily detract from the finest renderings of the bird and the young ones. Fences, buildings, distant tree trunks or branches which cut across the picture in such a manner as to distract the viewer—all these may have to be avoided. If this is impossible then the nest is unsuitable unless special considerations are overriding.

### Getting the Hide to the Nest

Having found the right site the next task is to get the hide into the correct position. This has to be done by accustoming the birds gradually to its presence. There are two ways to go about this—either you can build it full size some distance away and then

GANNETS ON GRASSHOLM. Gannets breed in colonies on several small rocky islands off the coast; in addition to Grassholm other well-known places to find them are Ailsa Craig, the Bass Rock, and St. Kilda. This picture illustrates the use of swing back with a camera of large negative size; by inclining the camera back so that the top is farther from the lens than the bottom a position can be found where all points in a receding plane are simultaneously in correct focus. This is valuable in obtaining maximum sharpness throughout the subject even when the prevailing light and the film speed enable the lens to be well stopped down; but it is even more so with colour films since these are slow and necessitate a wide aperture even in good light.—*Photo*: Eric Hosking.

SPARROW-HAWK'S CLUTCH. The nest was awkwardly situated high in a tree against the trunk, so the viewpoint was necessarily from directly above as the camera had to be clamped to the trunk itself.—*Photo:* John Warham.

WATER-HEN'S NEST. This is an example of straightforward nest photography. The waterside site in a woody nightshade bine was readily accessible, and the camera was mounted on a stand for a time exposure.—*Photo:* John Warham.

COMMON WHITETHROAT. Birds usually have a fairly definite route to the nest, and the camera can often be trained on a favourite perch to obtain attractive portraits of them, as well as to record the food they are carrying.—*Photo:* John Warham.

WREN. This feathered mite with the loud voice perched on a stake each time it approached its nest, and the camera recorded it in a characteristic alert attitude.—*Photo:* John Warham.

SWALLOW FEEDING YOUNG. The swallow does not approach its nest from
perch to perch but swoops straight to it—and when the nestlings are well advanced
the parents may have to feed them whilst hovering. Therefore the procedure is all
action and the birds seldom present an opportunity for securing "posed" portraits. This series was obtained using speedflash and a 35 mm. miniature camera,
and illustrates the potentialities of both the small camera and flash technique.—
*Photos:* G. Schutzenhofer.

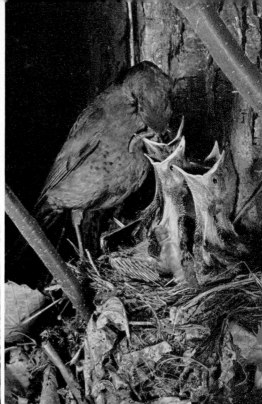

BLACKCAP SITTING (*opposite, top*). Both cock and hen take turns on the nest.—*Photo:* John Warham.

MALLARD SITTING (*opposite, bottom*). This is the duck; she will usually permit long exposures when incubating. The drake takes no part in domestic affairs.—*Photo:* John Warham.

COCK REED BUNTING (*above, left*). Adult birds can often be alerted by a click of the tongue to permit a slow shutter speed.—*Photo:* Eric Hosking.

HEN BLACKBIRD FEEDING YOUNG (*above, right*). Speedflash was used for this shot, and is a sure way of preventing blur due to movement of the subject.—*Photo:* Eric Hosking.

YOUNG SONG THRUSHES (*right*). Speedflash was also used for this picture. The camera was set up at 2½ ft. without a hide.—*Photo:* John Warham.

BLACKCAP FEEDING YOUNG CUCKOO. Parents continue feeding fledgelings after they leave the nest. The young may remain in one place sufficiently long to enable the camera to be trained on them and a series of pictures obtained as the parents make their rounds with food. The young cuckoo makes a particularly interesting subject, since it is not unknown for birds other than its foster-parents to assist in satisfying its voracious appetite. In Britain the commonest foster-parent is perhaps the meadow pipit, followed by the hedge sparrow and various small warblers.—*Photo:* Walter Wissenbach.

move it nearer by stages, or a small hide may be made at the spot where it will be finally required, and over a period of days enlarged until ready for use. Each method has its snags and advantages; frequently either may be feasible.

Erecting the hiding tent full-size and moving it gradually nearer entails more work than does the other method. Conversely, the birds get accustomed to the final shape and contour of the hide from the start, whereas with the second method the shape of the structure changes at each enlargement. Except when working in open places such as fields, heaths and moorlands, I prefer to build from small beginnings, and in many situations, for instance on cliffs and in trees, this is the only practicable solution.

Once it has been decided from which side the nest is to be viewed, a start is made by driving into the ground a few branches or short stakes—three will suffice—around which is fastened a small piece of fabric. A sack serves excellently. The whole is pinned firmly together and held in place by short flexible twigs stuck into the ground so that if a wind arises the material cannot flap about. Few things upset wild birds more than the flapping of canvas. Branches and bushes nearby may be waving violently but the vibrations of the hide may cause the greatest alarm, even desertion of the nest.

This first beginning will be perhaps 1½ to 2 feet high and about 1½ feet wide at the base. A few green sprays help to conceal it. Camouflaging of hides is seldom necessary for the bird's benefit; they will accept hides that contrast strongly with their surroundings, but it is always advisable in settled country to make the structure blend into its environment in order that it shall be less noticeable to casual observers. Suitable material for this purpose will usually be available on the spot, but care should be taken to see that bared branches are not left to call attention to your activities. Foliage should not be taken from close to the nest.

People often ask how long they should take to get the hide into position. This will vary greatly with the situation, the weather, the length of time the watcher has to devote to his hobby, and not least, the temperament of the birds themselves. With small birds like robins, warblers, finches and thrushes, which have young in their nurseries for only about fourteen days, it should be possible to get the hide in position within four days of commencing operations—and less than this time if you can move it twice daily, say in the morning and the afternoon, where the birds will permit this to be done. A hide should not be moved too late in the day lest the owner of the nest, upset by the change of scene, is prevented from returning before nightfall.

Ideally, with those species which rear their young in the nest, a start should be made when the eggs are on the point of hatching or have just done so. This will enable you to begin camera work before the young are more than a few days old, and at a period when the hen spends a great deal of her time in either brooding or tending the checks. The intervals between feeds are shorter too when the young are in their early stages of development, whilst at this time the parents are kept so busy that they often ignore the slight sounds made by shutters and draw-sheaths.

The ideal is often not possible, of course, and the part-time photographer may just not have the opportunity to begin according to the book. Instead he must do his hiding when he can, which may mean that his time for photography is limited, for young birds do not stay in their nests to suit our convenience. In any event it is undesirable to make any start until the eggs are believed to be about to hatch. This does not apply with those species such as gulls, plovers, waders generally, and terns, whose downy young run off the nest as soon as they are dry. These must necessarily be pictured on eggs if they are to be taken at the nest at all. With such

---

SETTING UP THE HIDE. The hide may be fully erected at a distance from the nest and then moved nearer day by day until it is in the required position. Another way is to erect it by degrees on the chosen site. First a few stakes or branches are draped with a sack (I). The next morning the erection is increased in size (2), and that evening or the next day it is replaced with the hide proper but only half covered (3). If all is well with the nest owners it may be completed after another 12–24 hours. It should be camouflaged against prying eyes, and a tell-tale path to it should be avoided (5). The nest is exposed as necessary for photography by "gardening" (6); some branches may be cut away provided sufficient cover remains; then this is tied back at the beginning of each session in the hide.

species hiding should not be started until incubation is reasonably well advanced.

A typical time-table for making a hide might be as follows:—

The nest containing small young having been found over the week-end, on Monday evening the first beginnings of a hide are started, on Tuesday enlarged to about half full-size, and possibly on the evening of the same day increased yet again. At this juncture it is a good idea to fasten a dummy lens to the front of the hide so that the birds get accustomed to the eye-like glint of glass. Such dummy lenses are easily made: a watch-glass can be mounted in a cardboard tube and tapes fastened on by which it can be pinned to the fabric; or the end of a round-bottomed bottle can be poked through the canvas and secured by a piece of string tied from the neck to the front cross-wire. I use an old R.R. lens for the purpose. When the birds have accepted the third enlargement of the hide and the dummy lens, the structure may then, on Wednesday, be brought to full height and pegged down.

Where the subjects' reactions to hiding are doubtful it is a sound practice to watch the adults' behaviour with binoculars from a distance. Should the parents prove frightened and obviously most reluctant to return, the hide must be dismantled and either set up farther away (to be moved up later as already described) or another more cautious attempt made at erecting the hide on the spot where it will finally be needed. When the birds prove abnormally shy the hide should be removed and the birds left to their own devices.

The working distance of the hide from the nest is governed by the size of the bird, its shyness, the focal length of the lens to be used and the size of the image required on the negatives. In the section "Guide to British Birds" are given recommended distances at which some of the commoner birds may be worked to obtain images on the negatives of about $1\frac{1}{2}$ in. for 8 in. lenses, $1\frac{1}{4}$ in. for $6\frac{1}{2}$ in. lenses, and $\frac{5}{8}$ in. (15-16 mm.) for 35 mm. cameras —the bird being considered as broadside on to the camera for the purpose of the calculations.

A hide placed too close to the nest means that the bird will appear too large on the negative. Ample surroundings should be included for several reasons. In the first place, although a close-up of the subject may make an attractive addition to a series, it is desirable to show something of the habitat in which the bird is nesting. Secondly, one can seldom be sure just where the bird will alight and what route it may take, and the greater the area covered the better the chance of obtaining pictures without lopping off the bird's tail. Most bird photographs are enlargements of only portions of the negatives.

Note that the completion of hide building precedes any adjustment to the surroundngs of the nest. In most instances it is hoped that the beginner will choose the most open sites possible so that little gardening is needed. Robins, thrushes and many other common kinds often fit the bill in this respect, though of course all will nest in deep cover and in unsuitable places.

## "Gardening"

With the hide accepted by the birds the delicate operation of opening up must be done if this is really necessary. The foliage must be so adjusted that the camera has an unimpeded view. Sometimes nests are situated so that the slight adaptations required may be done immediately before the first session—the branches or other obstruction being tied back with string or wire and released again when the day's photography is over. Where more alterations are called for they should be done by stages. It is usually possible to arrange things so that there is a certain amount of foliage at the front which can be adjusted by tying back at the last minute.

Nothing should be removed that can be fastened out of the way, and if branches have to be cut this must be done so that bare ends are not visible from the camera position; raw ends can sometimes be toned down by rubbing earth upon them. Apart from seeing that the birds do not suffer from the "gardening" and that the stability of the nest is not endangered (some warblers site their basket-like homes very carelessly), the important thing is to make sure that trimming is not obvious. Broken bents and stems with dying leaves go with bad workmanship and should be avoided like the plague. As a matter of fact, considerable skill may sometimes be needed in arranging the surroundings so that the final result is both pleasing and natural, perhaps even pictorial. Tied back foliage is released at the end of each turn in the hide so that the birds' privacy is restored. If necessary extra branches may be positioned to replace foliage that has been removed.

### The First Session

If your memory is as poor as mine it is a sound idea to keep inside the camera case a list of the items regularly needed on a "birding" outing. Before leaving home a check can be made against this to ensure that nothing has been overlooked. When you have come out prepared for a day's photography it is maddening to discover, when all set to begin work, that the cable release is missing. A check-list, if used, insures against such disappointments.

Setting up the camera for the first time at a nest generally takes longer than it does on subsequent occasions, and it is important to remember that while you are doing this the parent birds are being kept from their eggs or young, as the case may be. Thus the quicker you can get installed the less the danger for the birds and the sooner they settle down to their normal routine again. To keep such disturbance to a minimum the bird photographer should work out a "drill" for setting up, a definite sequence of steps to be carried out in a logical order. The kind of thing I have in mind is given on page 64 and this should be adapted to suit your own conditions and requirements.

This breakdown of events is not as formidable as it might appear at first sight and the following notes may be helpful:—

1. *Complete "gardening"*. The rule is to "under-garden" rather than to do too much, for presently a check will be made on the focusing screen to see if the opening up is adequate or whether further adjustments are needed. If the day is cold and the nestlings are small it is a sensible precaution to cover them with a handkerchief or a cap so that they do not become chilled. They are even more endangered by direct sunlight, and it is wrong to attempt

photography at nests where small young have to be exposed to strong sunlight. Such sites are unsuitable for photography, at least at the time of day during which sun beats down upon them, and in any event harsh lighting gives contrasty and unpleasant pictures. The gaping of adult birds as they shade their chicks from the heat is a distressing sight both in nature and in a print, though in tropical countries it is commonplace among birds whether they nest in the open or in the shade.

2. *Place something to focus on.* It is a good plan to put something at the nest on which you can focus and which indicates the expected position of the parents when they feed the chicks. It is important that this device, which may be a twig, a matchbox or anything else that is handy, should indicate the point at which the parents' heads are likely to be, as it is essential, whatever else may be out of focus, that the head and eyes are quite sharp. On subsequent sessions, when the place where the birds normally stand has been noted, it will be possible to place the focusing device with greater accuracy.

3. *Erect Tripod.* The tripod should be erected so that it is quite firm—the legs being pressed into the ground if necessary—and high enough to bring the camera to bear on the nest—about one or two feet above it. It should be arranged so that it occupies the least possible space inside the hide. The best arrangement is to push one leg forward out of the hide through a slit in the canvas about nine inches from the ground, and to splay the other two sideways and backwards so that you can sit in between them.

4. *Fasten on tilting top.* Since the camera is to look down slightly at the nest, the tilt top should be turned until the hinge is towards it, opened a little and clamped firm.

5. *Mount camera.* After fastening on, the camera is erected and turned so that the lens points forward roughly in the direction of the nest.

6. *Fit lens hood and push through canvas.* Do not be afraid to cut into the material—the hide will be full of holes by the end of the season anyway and yet may still have years of hard wear before it. The hole should not, however, be too large. A vertical slit is

63

# DRILL FOR SETTING UP CAMERA IN HIDE

| *Step* | *Points to Note* |
|---|---|
| 1. Complete "gardening". | Do this with care. Cover young if cold. |
| 2. Place something to focus on. | The object (matchbox for example) to be in expected position of bird's head. |
| 3. Erect tripod. | One leg forward, two to rear. Set it higher than nest so that camera points down. |
| 4. Fasten on tilting top. | Hinge towards nest. |
| 5. Mount camera. | Adjust roughly in direction of nest. |
| 6. Fit lens hood and push through canvas. | Alter tripod position if necessary. Make sure there are no obstructions in front of lens. |
| 7. Arrange subject on focusing screen. | Nest should appear below centre of picture. Adjust tilting top as required. |
| 8. Check "gardening" on focusing screen. | Subject area should look natural and background satisfactory. |
| 9. Focus. | Focus accurately on object placed for purpose, using a magnifier. Note definition of foreground and background and use swing back if necessary. |
| 10. Make exposure reading. | Also make reading of ground behind hide as guide if light changes during session. |
| 11. Set shutter and stop. | Select optimum combination for exposure reading, also taking into account depth of field required. |
| 12. Check shutter working. | Make sure working parts free from obstructions. |
| 13. Check peepholes. | Make sure they are adequate for good vision with comfortable posture. |
| 14. Set out slides, note-book, food, etc. | Make sure they are immediately accessible. |
| 15. Check hide from outside. | Hide must be completely opaque. Make sure camouflage well clear of lens. Remove focusing object. |
| 16. Get settled in hide. | Make sure you are thoroughly comfortable. |
| 17. Send off companion. | Make sure he knows time to return. |

perhaps best and the material should not be drawn taut against the hood or movements of the fabric may lead to camera shake.

7. *Arrange subject on focusing screen.* It will be found that the best position for the nest is for it to lie on the intersection of the lower-third of the negative and the central vertical line. If it is subsequently found that the parents habitually perch on the front rim of the nest, then the camera will have to be adjusted accordingly and so will the focus. Usually the birds tend to approach and feed the young from the sides of the nest or from the rear facing the camera.

8. *Check "gardening" on focusing screen.* In step (1) it was emphasized that excessive opening up should be avoided. Now, having roughly focused, it can be seen on the screen what odd leaves may need adjusting. Watch for glaring grasses and twigs and for shiny leaves acting like small mirrors and remove them if possible. The final result should look quite natural. Care should be taken to see that everything is firmly tied back so that if a breeze develops nothing can spring across the nest at a time when nothing can be done about it. The background should also be checked to see if the bird is going to be shown against any undesirable feature, and if so the offending object is removed or the camera angle changed to avoid it. With some small birds a backcloth can sometimes be used behind the nest, but it is seldom very satisfactory. Out-of-focus blobs of light are often an irritation. In bushy situations, out-of-focus blobs of this kind may be eradicated by filling up the far side of the bush with brushwood.

9. *Focus.* A step to be done with special care if disappointments are to be averted. Until there has been an opportunity of watching the birds from the hide you do not know just where they choose to stand when feeding, but as already pointed out, most of them prefer to perch at the rear of the nest and the camera should be focused on this assumption. Ideally the aim should be to get the foreground within the band of sharp focus and the background well out, so that the whole of the nest from the front almost to the rear is crisp and the bird itself stands out against the soft background. It is perhaps safest to focus (at full aperture) on a point slightly forward of the centre of the nest, since on stopping down

the depth will extend a greater distance to the rear of the point of sharpest definition than in front of it. A focusing magnifier is an asset as an aid to accuracy.

The swing back may be needed to get the foreground sharp without losing sharpness towards the back of the nest where the bird is expected to stand. The effect of swing back is simply to obtain sharpness on an oblique plane through the subject. There is a danger here, for it is very easy to get the nest and the bird's body beautifully sharp only to find later that the head was too far forward and lacks crispness. It is for this reason that the stick or other mark set up as a guide should indicate where the bird's head is expected to come. Swing back leads to some distortion, but the small amount involved is usually quite unnoticeable on the resulting print.

Many birds will perch both at the front and at the rear of their nests; often one of a pair regularly stands and feeds at the front and the other at the rear. Although the ideal may be to have so much depth of field that all these positions are covered, this is seldom possible in practice, and it may be desirable to adjust the focus quickly and accurately, now for the front and now for the rear of the nest. This can be done by fixing adjustable stops to the focusing rack so that when the bellows are extended to bring the front of the nest into focus one stop contacts a fixed vertically placed peg on the baseboard and further extension is impossible; a second adjustable stop on the other side of the camera works similarly when the bellows are contracted and the rear of the nest is covered. The rack is thus only able to move within the limits of the pegs, and you can switch from one point of focus to the other at a turn of the screw.

10. *Make exposure reading.* Since the light can vary so much in the course of a couple of hours and can easily be misjudged from within the hide, it is advisable to take readings of the nest under several light conditions if possible, before going inside. This is specially necessary if there are clouds in the sky. It is usually possible to check changes of light from within the hide. By leaving the back of the hide slightly open at the bottom the meter can be

used to get a reading on the ground; if this is subject to the same lighting conditions as the nest, then a fairly accurate idea will be obtained of the variation in exposure needed.

11. *Set shutter and stop.* At this stage a decision must be made based on your knowledge of the species concerned, aided by the section "Guide to British Birds", as to how long the bird is likely to stand still, and hence the slowest shutter speed likely to meet with success. With birds like robins and thrushes exposures of as long as a second are quite practicable; others, titmice for instance, are difficult to stop even when the Luc is worked at its fastest speed of about 1/40 sec. With an 8 in. lens a stop of at least *f*11 is usually necessary and *f*16 is much better at normal working distances. With practice it is possible to alter the stop merely by observing the size of the aperture from the rear of the camera with the back removed and the shutter open.

12. *Check shutter working.* The shutter should be worked a few times to see that all is well and that the release is free from defects. With Compound and Compur types check that the various levers are clear of the canvas. This can be ensured by having a piece of card with a hole in the centre into which the lens hood fits tightly. The card prevents the fabric from touching the shutter at all and also enables the operator's fingers to reach the controls without the bird seeing them.

13. *Check peepholes.* Now that the camera is set up the stool should be positioned and a check made that there is a peephole giving an adequate view of the nest, its surroundings and preferably of the birds' expected lines of approach. Such peepholes need not be more than one or two inches across; the material should be cut along three sides of a rectangle and the resulting tongue of canvas pinned back. If at a later date this particular peephole is not needed then it can be pinned into its original position again. One or two peepholes should also be made at the sides so that an all-round view is obtained. Such a wide field of vision is helpful in allowing the birds to be seen before they actually arrive at the nest; not all species advertise their whereabouts by song or by the rustle of their wings.

14. *Set out slides, notebook, food etc.* You should be properly organized within the hide—everything in its place, and a place for everything—so that when seconds count the time taken in changing slides, in refocusing, or whatever may be called for by the exigencies of the moment, is kept to a minimum. Perhaps a caution here may be timely regarding sandwiches. They should never be packed in greaseproof paper for the rustle of paper is, of all sounds, the one birds seem to detest most. Sandwiches should be wrapped in a serviette or cloth.

15. *Check hide from outside.* This is done to see that none of the camouflage can blow across the lens and as a final check on the opacity of the material; if any doubt exists on the latter an extra piece of fabric can be pinned to the interior of the hide wherever it may be needed.

16. *Get settled in hide.* Before going in this time any focusing device or covering over the young should be removed. Make certain you are comfortable; the seat should be firm, the shutter set, the dark slide in position and the sheath withdrawn.

17. *Send off companion.* It is often essential to have a helper who will fasten the hide up behind you, walk ostentatiously away when you are ready, and return at the end of an agreed period. This will generally deceive the parent birds, who have been watching all that has taken place, into believing the coast clear. Crows, jays and magpies, which are high on the evolutionary scale, are not taken in so easily, and two or more people should walk away from the hide when you are tackling these wily creatures. If only a single companion is available, he or she may deceive the birds success-fully by holding a coat or a piece of sacking at arm's length to simulate a second person.

Bird photographers often work in pairs; others prefer to work single-handed, getting farmers, gamekeepers and their sons, or other interested persons to see them in or out of their hides. Often long-suffering wives perform this valuable duty. The photo-grapher should arrange either for a definite time for relief (watches being synchronized) or for some signal to be made by him (such as showing a white handkerchief out of the corner of the hide) when he wishes the helper to return. In the event of the relief time coinciding with a long awaited visit by the bird or the occurrence of a particularly interesting episode, the helper, seeing no signal, keeps well away and so permits the episode to be recorded or observed as desired.

### Taking the Photographs

A long or short wait may be necessary before either bird returns; how long will depend to some extent on the care with which the hide was built and the trimming of the nest surroundings carried out. At first the birds will probably be hesitant, making several abortive attempts at alighting; even though they have taken a tantalizingly long time to come back you should not make any exposure on their first visit. Rather let them feed the young and get settled down before beginning photography. If they feed the nestlings very frequently they should be permitted to make several visits, and this will give you an opportunity to see where they perch and to make any last minute adjustments to the focus.

Only when the birds have overcome their nervousness after the disturbance associated with your recent activities should photography commence. If one of the adults settles down to brood a picture of this will present no difficulty, and quite long exposures may be given at such times; but watch for the slight movements as the bird breathes and time your exposure accordingly. At the first faint click of the shutter the bird will very likely shoot up its head and peer at the hide. Make no attempt to change plates, wind on the film or reset the shutter until the tension has subsided and the bird is again relaxed. Gradually both of them will become used to the quiet sound of the Luc and other noises, and they may even be "broken in", so to speak, by quietly clicking the tongue, making the noise louder by degrees until this and the sound of the shutter are ignored.

Some subjects become fantastically indifferent to noises. I remember a pair of bullfinches which were absolutely unperturbed by any sound from the hide, which was only four feet from the nest. Singing, shouting, whistling were all completely disregarded and injunctions to "stand still" and similar foolish demands were contemptuously ignored. Yet again, other birds may never become reconciled to the slight sounds that must inevitably accompany photography. When really difficult sitters are encountered it is generally wisest to give them best since the bird's welfare should receive the first consideration.

Birds with young to feed are best taken after the food has been disposed of and the chicks have subsided a little. Otherwise you may get a beautifully crisp study marred by a blurred mass of waving young in the foreground. After feeding, most small birds will pause intently to see if the chicks will eject any droppings, and this is the time to press the release. The droppings are picked up in the parent's bill and discarded when some distance from the nest.

Many species are still only for fractions of a second, and with such birds successful results depend largely on the cameraman's ability to anticipate these pauses and to press the release at the right moment. Once having begun to apply pressure it is no good drawing back when the bird appears about to move again. Probably a faint image will already have been recorded and when a second exposure is made this will be ruined by the ghost image superimposed upon the main one.

Although the restless bird is a teaser, when taking those species which are less rapid in their movements and using slow shutter speeds, it will be found that there is a tendency to snap the shutter closed too soon; in your eagerness to complete the exposure before the bird moves it is very tempting to underexpose. Often you may feel that movement must have spoiled the results and usually these fears are confirmed in the darkroom, but occasionally the negatives far surpass expectations. With the more phlegmatic birds like thrushes and robins for instance, a high percentage of the pictures should be free from movement. Your successes increase as you learn to anticipate the birds' intentions and to judge, almost by instinct, when to squeeze the release.

Pictures taken when the bird's head is turned directly towards

71

the camera or completely away from it, so that neither eye is visible, are generally unsatisfying. So are those in which the bird appears strained and on edge—a sign of inadequate preparation on the photographer's part. The eye should be obvious and the head more or less broadside on to the lens. With ground nesting kinds the arrangement of the eggs often governs the angle at which the bird incubates. By observing how she sits it is usually possible for the photographer to arrange the eggs for himself so that she will settle down broadside on to the camera. The method works well with plovers, stilts, terns and gulls and often with nightjars and stone curlews, most of which lay only two eggs.

It is desirable, though not always possible, to get a high-light in the eye, and in many cases where focusing has been accurate the image of the hide or some tree silhouetted on the skyline will be visible in the bird's eye.

Some birds are continually on the jitter; they nod their heads or wag their tails. The secret of overcoming such movements lies in making the exposure at the moment when the moving part of the bird's anatomy is about to change direction. Things get more complicated when both head and tail are in motion at the same time. It is then best to concentrate on eliminating head movement, trusting to luck that the wagging tail does not show. Possibly many exposures will have to be made before perfection is achieved; in any event the head and eye must be sharp.

Another tricky situation arises when both birds are together at the nest, since if one bird is still the other will probably be on the move. You have to take a chance here and either concentrate on the bird occupying most of the picture or try to look at the scene as a whole and trip the shutter when, for a moment, all seems still. Clearly the faster the shutter speed the greater the likelihood of a satisfactory result.

You will certainly meet with subjects which, like my bull-finches, become so accustomed to the sounds you make that they simply ignore the hide, and sometimes with birds that cannot be induced to remain motionless for a second. A sibilant noise from the lips, or a sharp click of the tongue, will usually make most birds pause just long enough for an instantaneous exposure; but with very tame sitters it may be necessary to put a finger out of the hide to attract attention and create the opportunity you need. A white feather twirled round slowly sometimes does the trick, but when I tried this dodge with one pair of long-tailed titmice the birds simply flew at the hide, hovered before the peephole and tried, apparently out of sheer curiosity, to peer inside.

Taking down the camera and packing up does not usually take long. Once again cover the chicks if the weather is cold, and it is most important before leaving to slacken off twigs and vegetation which have been tied out of the way. The nest must be adequately screened when the hide is unoccupied and additional foliage provided if necessary. The hide must be securely fastened up and the dummy lens replaced, while branches should be pressed into the sides if the situation is an exposed one and likely to be windy.

## Perches

After a few sessions it will soon be observed that each bird of a pair prefers to use a definite route when it comes in and when it leaves. By noting just where each perches a series of pictures showing the birds away from the nest can be obtained. It will often be impossible to use existing perches without making some adjustments, and many kinds will readily take to a perch provided by the photographer. Nightingales, warblers, chats, titmice and owls will all oblige in this way providing the perch is correctly placed. It should be set up to lie in the normal path of the bird as it comes to the nest. Any competing resting places should be removed if possible. Once it has become accustomed to using the perch the bird is likely to continue to do so on subsequent occasions.

It is important to select perches carefully; they must be appropriate to the species concerned and should look entirely natural. Some time may have to be spent in finding just the right one for a given situation. When focusing remember that the bird's head will probably come slightly forward of the perch and this should be allowed for.

Sometimes, when a nest is unsuitable for direct photography

through being too deeply hidden in foliage, badly illuminated or unsatisfactory for any other reason, it is possible to take the birds as they pass to and fro by focusing on a favoured perching place where conditions are better than at the nest itself.

### Compound, Compur, Prontor Shutters

So far this chapter has been mainly concerned with shutters of the silent type. Where Compound, Compur or Prontor types are employed a few additional factors must be considered. If the sitter is of a staid temperament and habitually remains motionless for as long as a second at a time, try the shutter on the "Brief" setting. Robins, nightingales, pigeons, ducks and others will stand still long enough for this method to succeed and at "Brief" such shutters are as silent as the Luc. Otherwise you have to reckon with the extra movements associated with recocking the shutter after each exposure. And once the shutter has been set at a given speed it cannot be altered very easily when sitting behind the camera. A small mirror such as dentists use for peering behind one's teeth is helpful for reading the figures from behind. To help in resetting the shutter I fasten a short length of thin nylon fishing line to the reset lever so that by pulling on this the shutter is cocked.

In addition to the extra noise made by these shutters as compared with those of the silent type—noise which is not confined to the closure of the blades, so that some birds may start at the first sound and spoil the exposure—there is also the slight click made as the reset lever is moved into the ready position. With cautious birds a decent interval should be allowed to elapse after taking a photograph before resetting in readiness for the next one. Despite these several disadvantages many birds will accept shutters of this kind, but a little more care and patience is needed when using them than if a silent type only is employed.

### Working Single-handed

Much emphasis has been placed on the need to consider the birds' well-being when working at the nest, and for this reason, if for no other, the assistance of a companion to see you in and out of hides has been advocated. But sometimes such a companion is just not available . . . when and how may a helper be dispensed with?

Most small birds nesting in bushy places where there is a good deal of cover are not unduly critical of hides which have been properly introduced by stages, and many birds return readily to their nests when all movement has ceased in the vicinity. In these circumstances a companion *may* be unnecessary. Every bird is an individual, however—no two react exactly in the same way to a given situation; one robin may be confiding, the next quite the reverse. So if you do try to work alone the attempt should be abandoned if the birds prove undeceived by your disappearance.

Nor should it be overlooked that your exit is no less important than your manner of entering the hide; sudden emergencies should be avoided. Sometimes it is possible to slip out unobserved when the old birds are away feeding; at other times when either parent is at the nest it may be sufficient to mutter softly and, by increasing the loudness of the voice, to cause the bird to move away and give you a chance to come out quietly. It may even be possible to creep out of the back of the hide while the bird is still at the nest. To do this successfully involves crawling on all fours; every move must be planned in advance so that your departure is noiseless and the hide must be kept between you and the bird. Much depends on the lie of the land, whether the off-duty bird is likely to be about, and on your subject's temperament whether such a method would be permissible. One of my early sitters was a tufted duck nesting on a sedge-covered ridge in an old gravel pit. Duck are difficult and shy creatures at the best of times and this bird was no exception, yet it was possible by opening the back of the hide to squirm away along the ridge without putting her off the eggs.

There are certain birds which regularly absent themselves from their nests for long periods. Where such nests are in woods or similar cover you can usually get installed during the owners' absence and, likewise, after a feed you can come out when there is no sound of the birds in the vicinity. Doves and pigeons fall into this category, for they leave their squabs between feeds for up to four hours at a stretch. Other kinds, hawks and eagles, for instance, although allowing long periods to elapse between visits, have such keen eyes and wide horizons that the entering of a hide unattended merely invites failure.

Working single-handed is most often necessary, perhaps, when you are working with owls after dark. Someone may be cajoled into seeing you in of an evening, but when it comes to arranging for a relief at one o'clock in the morning there is seldom a rush of volunteers. This snag can usually be overcome with the help of about forty feet of rope. One end is left inside the hide and to the other is tied a bundle of sticks or a weighted sack. This is placed on the ground well away from the hide so that it can drag freely through the undergrowth without getting entangled. The idea is that when you wish to pack up, by pulling steadily on the rope the sack is drawn along the ground making a noise at some distance from the hide, a noise that gradually gets louder and closer. The owl will hop to her entrance hole, will peer down towards the sound and will depart to watch events from a perch near by. The sack is then drawn right up into the hide and to the accompaniment of a little singing perhaps, and flashing of torches, you dismantle the equipment and depart leaving the sack inside. The same dodge can be used when a ground hide is employed.

### On Taking a Chance

Some of the most notable and unusual pictures of birds have been the reward of the cameraman's prompt and competent reaction to lucky opportunities. The bird photographer should be on the alert for the unusual and not afraid of taking a chance. The bird may be too near or too far away for correct focus, and a quick turn of the focusing screw by estimation, followed by pressure on the release, are needed before the chance has gone for ever. Sometimes the subject may be perfectly posed but outside the field covered by the lens. Then the temptation to swing the camera on to the bird may be irresistible. Any such movement must be done with agonizing care and the traverse must be so gradual that the bird cannot detect it—or it must be made when its head is turned the other way. The odds are that the bird will walk away or fly off just as the picture is about to be taken, but sometimes such chances come off.

One of my favourite photographs—of a turtle dove in song—was made in a similar manner. Shy though these seldom-pictured birds are, it was possible to swing the camera on to the bird as it stood calling quietly to itself, to focus accurately upon it and to make a series of exposures before the bird flew to its nest nearby. Some incidents are accompanied by so much movement that, without the aid of electronic flash, it seems hopeless even to attempt to record them. Nevertheless chance shots may occasionally prove successful, as on another occasion with a turtle dove when the movements of the squabs whilst being fed were so violent that the chance of getting a satisfactory record seemed remote indeed, yet a picture was obtained.

*Bird Series*

No two bird photographers have exactly the same angle on their hobby; some wish merely to obtain good portraits of their subjects, others try to produce studies of a particular species covering as wide a range of activities as possible. And there is much to be said in favour of a fine series of a single bird, whether common or rare. Such a series might cover some or all of the following facets of bird behaviour:—

1. The building of the nest.
2. Close-up of the nest and eggs.
3. Nest and eggs shown in relation to the environment.
4. Parent(s) incubating.
5. Change-over at the nest.
6. The hatch.
7. Newly-hatched young.
8. Well-feathered young.
9. Parent(s) brooding.
10. Parent(s) asleep on the nest.
11. Feeding of the brooding hen by the male.

77

12. Parents feeding the chicks.
13. The young doing their wing exercises.
14. The young preening.
15. Nest sanitation.
16. Family party after the young have flown.
17. The old birds perched appropriately showing plumage or other sex differences.
18. Adult birds feeding in typical surroundings.
19. Flight studies at the nest.
20. Flight studies of the flocks.
21. Reaction to enemies.
22. Courtship displays.
23. Distraction and disablement displays.
24. Drinking, bathing, sunbathing.
25. Roosting.
26. Castings ejected.
27. The hides used, etc.

This is not an exhaustive list, though it may seem formidable enough, nor is it appropriate to all species. "Castings ejected", for example, could hardly apply to a redshank, since, as far as I know, the bird does not eject the hard parts of its food in the form of pellets—a habit more or less confined to owls, hawks and gulls. Nor would "Change-over at the nest" apply to a duck as the males do not take any part in incubation.

It will be realized that to assemble a series of pictures covering anything like the above range of habits would be quite a tall order, would involve working at a number of nests, and could only be covered over several years, even if the subject chosen were a familiar one like the robin, or a stout-hearted one like the long-tailed tit.

A bird series need not be limited to a collection of photographs depicting the habits of one particular kind. An equally interesting and valuable series might show a single aspect of bird behaviour as revealed in a wide variety of species. A set of pictures of birds in their roosts might be made—or any other habit that took your fancy. There would be plenty of scope for ingenuity and photographic skill.

# More Difficult Sites

HAVING SUCCEEDED IN portraying some of the commoner species from the confines of a ground hide, the photographer will presently wish to tackle birds at nests which are less conveniently placed. In this chapter some of the more important situations likely to be encountered are considered.

## Pylon Hides

The standard ground hide can only be used with nests not higher than about five feet, or at the most seven feet, even if specially long uprights are used, extensions fastened to the tripod legs, and a box used to stand on. When taller situations have to be worked a pylon hide is usually the solution. Basically this consists of four uprights—probably taken from live timber (with the owner's permission)—which are sunk a little into the ground and braced together by smaller boughs fastened on by nails. The framework of such a hide is shown on page 95.

The bracing is done from the bottom upwards, and when a height is reached which will allow the camera to look down slightly into the nest, straight struts are fixed to carry a board drilled with holes for $\frac{1}{4}$ in. Whitworth screws to secure the camera; a tripod is dispensed with in pylon hides. Providing plenty of holes are made in the board (which should be about 4 in. wide by $\frac{1}{2}$ in. thick) a satisfactory position for camera and tilt-top is readily found. A similar pair of bearers are nailed two or three feet lower and carry another board to form a seat. A few struts fastened diagonally, and guy ropes from the top, make the contraption stable. The upper portion is covered with canvas and several pieces fastened in position with roofing felt tacks will be found more convenient than a standard covering. A footrest should be provided.

Such a hide cannot be built all at once. Apart from the risk of scaring the birds, the time needed would be so great that there would be a grave danger of the chicks or eggs coming to harm. Probably work spread over the evenings of a whole week would be required, the poles and spars being collected and carried to the site before beginning building. The canvas covering is introduced piece by piece, though this may be commenced before the framework is complete. At first the latter will seem flimsy and inadequate; as it becomes braced so it gains in strength. If needed, spars can be nailed from the uprights to adjacent trunks to increase stability. The introduction of the dummy lens and the arrangement of the nest surroundings follow the usual pattern. Several nails should be provided for hanging coats and camera cases inside and a shelf is often useful.

Such hides are necessary for most nests from six to thirty feet high. Above such heights the work involved becomes very considerable. In siting pylons care should be taken to build so that the top comes at the correct distance from the nest, for alteration after completion will be very difficult.

*Tree-top Nests*

When attempting to work nests in the tops of trees the first difficulty is to find a suitable site which can be overlooked from a position in the same or an adjacent tree. For example, in a rookery many of the nests will be seen to be at the very tops of the trees where hide building is impossible. With patience, however, a likely looking nest may be discovered. It will be necessary to climb the tree (climbing irons come in useful here) to size up the possibilities. If judged suitable some spars must be brought to the site, hauled aloft and then fixed by nails, ropes or wire among the branches at a point where there are sufficient limbs to support a framework, and from which a satisfactory view of the nest is given. From these first spars the beginnings of a framework are

HERON. Most birds that obtain their livelihood in watery places nest on the ground or among the sedges and reeds. But not fisherman heron, who prefers communal life in a "heronry" in the tops of tall trees. This picture was obtained from a 60-ft. portable pylon hide designed and constructed of tubular steel by the photographer.—*Photo:* H. Auger.

TWO ROOKS (*opposite, top*). Taken from a tree-top hide this picture illustrates the importance of giving a sufficiently long exposure with dark-plumaged birds. —*Photo*: John Warham.

SPARROW-HAWK SITTING (*opposite, bottom*). A pylon hide was necessary for this wary subject.—*Photo*: John Warham.

TREE CREEPER (*above, left*). This confiding little bird of the tree trunks usually sites its nest high enough to warrant a pylon hide.—*Photo*: Eric Hosking.

GREEN WOODPECKER AND YOUNG (*above, right*). Taken from a pylon hide about 25 ft. high. Out-of-focus patches in the background can be toned down by local fogging during enlarging.—*Photo*: John Warham.

MERLIN (*left, top*). This small hawk is a bird of the wild moorlands of Wales and the west country, and nests on the ground among the heather. The bird is shown perched at a vantage point a short distance from the nest. *Photo:* Eric Hosking.

LITTLE SHEARWATER (*opposite, top*). An example of photographing a nest below ground; the site was opened up and a false roof fitted. This picture was taken on Eclipse Island, S.W. Australia.—*Photo:* John Warham.

MARSH HARRIER (*left, bottom*). This bird is rather rare in Britain, and when it occurs favours the marshes and broads in the eastern counties. A quarter-plate reflex camera, with shutter specially speeded to 1/1500 sec., was used for this picture of the cock alighting with food.—*Photo:* Eric Hosking.

CHOUGH (*opposite, bottom*). A member of the crow family which favours the cliffs and mountains of the north-west and Ireland. This pair built their nest on a ledge in a quarry and were photographed by speedflash.—*Photo:* Harold Platt.

84

KINGFISHER WITH PREY (*above, left*). Since the nest is deep in a hole in the stream or river bank the camera has to be trained on a favourite perch to obtain pictures of this bird.—*Photo:* John Warham.

WATERHEN SITTING (*above, right*). Although one of the commoner British water-side birds the waterhen, or moorhen, is remarkably camera shy, and a co-operative one that will return to the nest when the hide is occupied may not be easy to find. —*Photo:* Eric Hosking.

GREAT CRESTED GREBE (*opposite, top*). In contrast to the waterhen this fine bird of the lakes and reservoirs is retiring by nature, yet it is a co-operative camera subject. The lower-than-normal viewpoint makes full use of the water as a background. —*Photo:* John Warham.

BLACK-HEADED GULLS (*opposite, bottom*). Another example of the use of the water as a background. The black—or rather, dark brown—head is a summer adornment only; it is white in winter.—*Photo:* Eric Hosking.

YOUNG AMERICAN EGRETS.
They have left the nest and are
waiting for the parents to return with food.—*Photo:* K. H.
Maslowski and P. Koch.

YOUNG GREEN HERONS.
They look awkward and un-
gainly, yet soon develop into
graceful birds.—*Photo:* L. M.
Chace.

made. This is gradually strengthened by the addition of further struts fixed to anything solid enough to hold them and when complete, canvas material is tacked into place. A ladder will be helpful, or a series of short and strong branches may be nailed at intervals of about two feet up the trunk, thus forming a ladder on the tree itself.

One of the big problems with tree-top hides is how to combat the wind. Not only does this flap the fabric and so scare sitting birds, but on some days photography may be impossible on account of the swaying of the branches around which the hide is fashioned. Thin laths or branches nailed to the sides (not to the front or back) after the covering has been fitted will help to keep movement to a minimum, especially if the fabric is fastened to them with drawing pins or tacks. Another good idea is to fix a spar to connect the branch bearing the nest to the main supports of the hide, so linking the motions of the nest and the hide and preventing the former from swinging in and out of focus. This arrangement has the obvious disadvantage that any movement of the hide will be reflected at the nest so that a sudden slip by the photographer could startle his quarry.

Hides in the tree-tops should be provided with a plank for a seat and a perforated board for mounting the cameras. A wooden floor is desirable, but if this cannot be fitted sacking should be spread underneath to prevent birds which settle lower down from seeing inside, and to act as a catching net in the event of any item of equipment being accidentally dropped.

When working high up like this it is a good plan to have a rope to which can be tied camera cases and other gear for hauling from ground level direct to the hide. The rope may come in useful too when wishing to deceive the old birds before settling down for a photographic session, for if a sack is tied on and lowered down to your helper who promptly walks away with it, the parents will generally return quite confidently. This overcomes the difficulty of having companions who cannot climb the tree themselves. The sack can also be hauled up to simulate the return of an assistant at the end of a session.

Tree-top hides must be built slowly, giving the birds ample time to grow accustomed to each addition, particularly when it comes to fixing the covering. Any gardening should be done before the hide is finished since it is often difficult to get to the nest once the structure is complete. With birds that use their tree-top homes year after year, such as rooks, egrets, herons, ibis and some eagles, it is quite possible to make the framework of the hide out of the breeding season when the birds are absent. When nesting has begun all that is then necessary is to fit the covering to the framework by stages. This method ensures the minimum of disturbance for the breeding birds, and much of the hard work can be done at a slack time of the year.

Tree-top nests on steep hillsides or in gullies can sometimes be viewed from the ground higher up, and possibly even photographed from ground hides. Usually a lens of long focal length (12 to 17 in.) will be needed as the distance between camera and subject is likely to be considerable.

### Nests on Cliffs and Crags

Hide work on cliffs and mountain crags is an invigorating but sometimes arduous pursuit. The nesting sites of birds that breed in colonies are usually easy to find once you have got to their haunts, and the clamour of voices and the busy aerial traffic of the adults are obvious clues to follow. On the other hand, the nests of solitary kinds like ravens, buzzards and eagles may take a lot of searching out, and many sites are too precipitous to offer much hope of hide making. When such a nest has been found, possible points from which it can be overlooked should be investigated. The use of a strong manilla rope is often a big help in reaching such vantage points from which you can weigh up the possibilities. If a suitable spot is found—bearing in mind the lighting and similar considerations—then it may be thought desirable to remove some of the rock in an effort to widen a platform to take the hide. A cold chisel and a hammer can sometimes work wonders where anything like a reasonable foothold already exists. On less steep slopes having a clothing of grass and thrift, uprights can often be forced into crevices and clefts. Then, by lavish bracing with guys, a hide of sorts may often be produced. If this has to be pitched on a steep slope two uprights on the lower side will suffice, for cross-pieces may be fixed to the tops of these and then forced into the ground on the higher side. It is surprising how, with a little ingenuity, quite unpromising places can be rendered comfortable and safe.

Note that this sort of work does not involve dangling precariously over cliffs on the ends of ropes. Usually these are only needed to give the climber additional support over awkward points or when carrying hides and heavy gear.

It is important to take precautions against anything being able to roll out of the hide. Camera cases should be tied to something firm, and sods can often be laid downhill to correct the slope. A board fixed between the lower uprights helps to increase stability.

Winds frequently howl fiercely along exposed cliffs and sods or rocks should be placed on the roof of the hide and all canvas pinned down securely. It is surprising how much a properly pegged-down hide can withstand. Recently I was working on a rocky island off the southern coast of Australia and exposed to all the winds that blew. One of my cliff-side hides successfully withstood wind speeds as high as 80 m.p.h. during gales which lasted for a week at a time.

Cliff nests are by no means always ideal photographically. In particular there is often a lot of out-of-focus rock on one side of the negative. Intelligent use of side swing will enable much of this to be brought into focus.

### Hole Nesting Birds

A variety of birds nest inside holes of one sort or another, in trees, in masonry, pipes, stone walls and earthy banks. Species using such places include many of the titmice, woodpeckers, storm petrels, owls and stockdoves. This method of breeding prevents pictures being taken at the nest itself and the camera has to be set up to cover the entrance hole. This may not be easy, for many birds like to fly straight into their holes and give few opportunities for pictures, except when they emerge and momentarily pause to look around before departing. Sometimes little can be done about this except to provide a convenient perch and to take the birds as they rest upon it. Titmice, owls and redstarts are often very obliging in this respect, but the perch must be carefully placed and alternative ones removed.

With woodpeckers and titmice greater opportunities exist when the young are well grown, for then they reach to the nest hole on their own account and the old birds remain at the entrance while they give out the food. There is less activity after the feed when the parent pauses to collect the excreta, and this is usually the best moment at which to press the release.

At tree-trunk nests due allowance must be made when focusing for the thickness of the bird, and some sort of focusing guide should be fastened by the nest hole to indicate the nearest point to the camera which must be sharp. A cigarette packet serves the purpose and the print on this makes accurate focusing easy. If the wall or trunk in which the hole occurs is vertical and the camera is set square to it, there will be no danger of an out-of-focus foreground, but with nests in tree trunks parts of the tree may be nearer to the camera than others. Side swing of the camera back will then be found invaluable.

When the hole is deep the nestlings may keep well back out of sight, so that you see nothing of them at feeding times and little of the parent except the end of the tail. This difficulty can be overcome by placing a stone or piece of wood at the back of the hole so that the young are brought forward into view.

The position of the hide in relation to the nest may be controlled by the surroundings and by the lighting. The camera may have to be placed directly in front of the hole, but where possible you will find that a position about half-way between a completely frontal viewpoint and a sideways one is best.

While some birds using tree-trunk cavities will reveal their secrets when the trunk is tapped—owls and stockdoves, for example—others sit tightly when danger threatens. When examining holes note the condition of the entrances. If cobwebs are spun across them then clearly no birds have been inside recently. Sometimes claw-marks plainly indicate the visit of an owl. Woodpeckers usually sit tightly. If the hole is within reach a small inclined mirror and a torch may enable you to look inside. At other times it may be necessary to retire some distance and watch events through binoculars. Many woodpecker-type holes prove on inspection to be "blind", and a useful check on the freshness of any excavations may be made by examining the ground below for tell-tale chippings. If the birds are suspected of boring, a cloth fastened firmly to the ground underneath will reveal any further chippings. By removing these from time to time you may discover when nest making has been completed.

Placing a thin twig or bent across the entrance to a nest-hole may furnish a clue as to whether it is occupied. If the obstruction has been moved on a later inspection it shows that something has been inside—although not necessarily a bird or one intent on nesting.

### Birds Below Ground

Several kinds of birds burrow into the ground when breeding and in certain cases it is possible to portray them inside the nesting chamber itself. I have done this with several kinds of petrels both in Britain and abroad by fitting the nests with false roofs. These were lifted at night and the birds photographed by flash from within a hide placed directly over the nesting chamber. Such a method can only be used with certain petrels which are nocturnal on their breeding grounds and which leave their chicks to their own devices during the hours of daylight. Thus the necessary excavations can be made without the adult birds being disturbed since they are miles away at the time. The entrance tunnel is not interfered with in any way so that, apart from the hide, the surroundings and landmarks remain unaltered. This procedure could not be used with an attentive species like the European kingfisher, but it might be possible with the puffin.

### Birds by Marsh and Lake

Some of the most fascinating birds are those which frequent

rivers, lakes and swamps, nesting in the coarse vegetation by the water's edge, on the water itself, or among the lush grasses of marshy areas. Waterside nests may often be overlooked from a hide placed on the bank, but where the nest is too far out the hide must be built in the shallows at the edge of the water. If the bottom is firm, as in most river beds, no special difficulties are encountered, but if, as often happens, there is much mud and silt, this may complicate matters. A large flat wooden board, say a yard square, may help to form a firm base resting on the mud, and long uprights can be driven into the bed of the lake around it. Planks may be needed to walk out to reach the hide without sinking in.

Maybe the only solution is a floating hide, built on a punt or a raft of timber or cans. These must be firmly anchored to the bed by means of stakes driven well in; otherwise camera shake may mar your pictures.

Essentially aquatic birds such as grebes, which seldom leave the water, may be photographed from behind a screen open at the back and with no roof; such hides are conveniently made from lake-side reeds. When attempting to show birds floating on water ruffled by the breeze, it is a good idea to make the exposures when the bird rises on the crest of a wavelet, since in this way pictures free from movement are more likely to be obtained.

Bird photography in marshy places where snipe, plover, wagtails and the like are probable sitters, offers little difficulty unless cattle have access to the area. If so the hide must be surrounded with an adequate barrier of posts and wire.

---

TREE, CLIFF AND WATERSIDE HIDES. A hide to cover a tree-nesting bird is built of a framework of stout timber nailed or lashed to branches of the tree and covered with hessian or canvas (1). Birds nesting in holes in trunks, or in flimsy tree-tops incapable of supporting a hide, necessitate the use of a pylon hide (3); this is built of timber uprights and cross struts, braced by guy lines. A portable hide can often be used on a cliff ledge by wedging the uprights into crevices (2); note that it may be possible to photograph a nest in a cliff-side tree from higher ground. A floating hide of hurdles and reeds can be built on a flat bottomed boat (4), and reeds make a good camouflage for the standard hide erected on the bank (5).

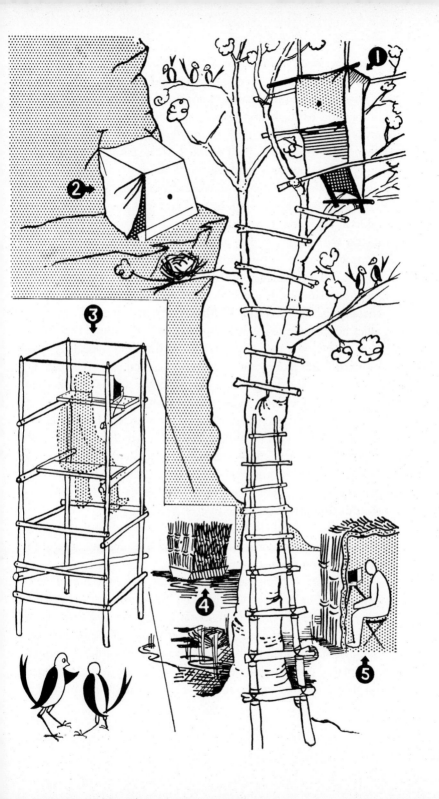

### Nests on Moors and Beaches

When working on moors, beaches and similar exposed places the wind may be a problem and it is usual to make hides as low as possible and to stack stones and turf around them to anchor the canvas securely. Hides may be made solely of stones or peat. When working on a slope it is worth while taking the trouble to dig into the slope and level off the floor of the hide. Otherwise it will be difficult to use the stool, and a kneeling position in such a cramped space leads to agony and cramp. Comfort is most desirable in any hide, for it enables you to concentrate on picture-making without being distracted by aches and irritations.

Searching for nests on moors must be largely a matter of observation from a distance coupled with your knowledge of the terrain. Moorland birds are very thin on the ground, and it will generally be found easier to discover nests along the sides of gullies bordering the streams than on the open tops.

On sea beaches, too, nests may be hard to find, especially those of solitary birds like oyster catchers and ringed plovers, which lay highly camouflaged eggs on pebbly foreshores. The presence and behaviour of the birds will give a clue as to where they are breeding, and the suspected area may be watched from behind a groyne or the grass of the dunes. Once all is quiet the birds usually return to their nests fairly readily. Those kinds which nest in colonies—terns for instance—are not so difficult to locate and once the breeding area has been found eggs are frequently so plentiful that they cannot be overlooked.

Beach hides are likely to be submitted to the vicissitudes of the wind, and they should be well guyed with stones laid around the bottom and on the roof.

With ground-nesting birds the tendency to use too high a viewpoint should be guarded against. The higher the camera position the greater the depth of field, but a bird portrayed so that too much of its back is shown looks neither natural nor attractive in a photograph. For such birds a short tripod is desirable, the camera being placed probably no more than two feet from the ground.

In addition to picturing the bird as it incubates and stands by its nest you may wish to make some shots as it stands several feet away from the eggs. First ascertain the normal lines of approach (ground-nesting birds, like other kinds, usually have well-worn routes to their nests) and then decide where the oncoming bird is to be photographed. A small stone is then placed at the spot as a guide. When the bird returns the release is pressed as it comes up to the mark; if necessary a click of the tongue may be given to make the bird pause long enough for the picture to be made. When attempting shots of this sort it may be helpful to use two cameras mounted on one tripod, one camera being trained on the eggs and the other on the bird's line of approach.

### Combating Winds

Winds can be an infernal nuisance. The birds may be extremely nervous if the hide is flapping about, and there is a danger of camera shake as the material pushes against the tripod and the lens panel. Winds are often strongest on open beaches, in sea-bird colonies around the cliffs, and on exposed islands. There are several ways to tackle the problem. Extra guys may be fitted. Ropes can be tied tightly round the sides and front (but not the back) both inside and out, thus restricting the movement of the canvas which may be pinned to the ropes. A very good answer involves the use of wire netting. A single piece as long as the combined lengths of the sides and the front of the hide and nearly as wide as its height is needed. The cover is removed, the netting folded to fit snugly against the uprights (leaving the back open, of course) and the cover and guy ropes replaced. The canvas can then be fixed to the netting with pins in as many places as may be necessary. On windy days there are usually momentary lulls, and it is during these that the pictures should, if possible, be taken.

### Some Unorthodox Hides

From time to time the keenness of individual photographers spurs them to undertake very difficult tasks and leads to the making of ingenious hides.

One of the most spectacular ideas was that of hanging a balloon basket over a Himalayan precipice in order to bring cameras to bear on an otherwise impossible site. This was the device adopted by Mrs. Illum Berg, the Swedish nature photographer, who took the first pictures of the bearded vulture at its nest in this way.

Pylons are necessary for high sites when there is no adjacent tree or other natural feature from which the nest can be overlooked. But very high sites require something more than the usual wooden affair made from local materials. Several workers have called upon the resources of builders and have had tubular scaffolds set up on which the hide has been placed. One of the most notable examples was the sixty-feet-high pylon used by Eric Hosking and Lord Alanbrooke when filming a Berkshire hobby at its nest. On the other hand, Harold Auger of Lincoln achieves the same results with less expenditure; he has designed and constructed from one-inch conduit a portable pylon hide having a maximum height of sixty feet. The whole can be carried by two people, and this worker's exquisite pictures of herons and rooks leave no room to doubt the effectiveness of the device.

A difficult problem faced Harold Platt and Arthur Brook when they set out to portray choughs at their nest inside a disused lead mine. The ledge on which the nest rested was in a vertical shaft where water dripped continuously, and in order to position the camera it was necessary to fasten it, together with the flash gear, on to the top of a telescopic tube. In this way the camera could be raised to the correct level, focusing having been carried out by prior estimation. The shutter and the flash were worked by remote control from below. Despite the fact that the whole apparatus had to be dismantled after each exposure, some excellent pictures were made—a just reward for hard work and enterprise.

Comdr. A. W. P. Robertson's "mobile" hide is an interesting departure from custom. This consists of a base-board, three feet square and hinged in the middle as shown on page 35. At the corners of the square are fixed four upright pegs on which the corner poles will fit snugly, and there are also holes in the base-board to allow it to be pegged securely to the ground. On this base-board the uprights, cross-wires and canvas covering are erected and the whole can be moved bodily from place to place.

If it is found just before the first session at the nest that the hide is too close or too far away, it is an easy matter to make the necessary alteration to the siting of it. Once it is correctly placed pegs can be put in and the guying done in the usual way. Such a hide seems to offer distinct possibilities when working in gull colonies, at sites where the hiding-tent is to be moved into position by stages, in sheltered areas where guying is not needed, and particularly with wary birds when the minimum of noise and disturbance is desirable during the hiding of the nest.

Cars can be useful as hides; birds will often ignore a vehicle and the people it contains so that sometimes the tripod can be rigged up inside and nesting birds photographed from within. There is also the possibility of using a car as a sort of roving hide. In Britain when driving along country roads you may often notice birds perched picturesquely on hedges and gate posts, birds that would make excellent studies could a camera be trained upon them.

# Birds—Wild and Free

So far only the easiest aspect of bird photography has been dealt with—their portrayal at the nest. Getting pictures of them away from the influence of the nest is more difficult for birds are the most volatile of creatures and success may only be possible after disappointments and discomforts.

### Birds in the Garden

Perhaps the most rewarding out-of-season work can be done in the garden. Characteristic studies of common birds like robins, starlings, sparrows (how few good pictures there are of these birds) and titmice can be obtained quite easily. The simplest method is to set up a feeding table beside a permanent hide. If the latter is a reasonably strong affair made of wood, roofing felt or similar material, it will prove more serviceable than the ordinary canvas hide designed for portability and temporary situations. Or the bird table may be placed before a garden shed or an outhouse inside which you can be concealed.

Local birds soon become familiar with such permanent hides and the dummy lens if food is regularly provided on the table. Given satisfactory lighting conditions, the main problem becomes one of getting the subject isolated from its fellows and in satisfactory surroundings. Photographs made at the bird table, or of birds picking up food from the ground, are not very attractive; the food is too obvious and unnatural. It is far better to arrange a suitable perch above or beside the feeding point on which your visitors may settle before dropping down for a meal. Such a perch can be changed when desired.

One way of getting garden birds to come to a perching post is to drill small holes on one side near the top. These should be about half an inch in diameter and depth and they are filled with fats, nuts and similar attractions. The post is set up so that the holes are away from the camera and not shown on the print. Once the birds have discovered the food and that it can be reached without their leaving the top, good opportunities for pictures are obtained.

In the winter, light is often a problem. Apart from the long exposures needed on grey days, the resulting negatives, even if sharp, tend to be rather flat. The best conditions are provided by winter sunlight, the softness of which is very suitable. Care should be taken when placing the hide to see that the background is unobtrusive and it may be necessary to rig up a backcloth to achieve this. The material should be light in colour, vaguely blotched with darker areas (preferably applied with a spray gun) and firmly fixed to a fence or other support so that the fabric cannot flap or sag. A backcloth should be put up well before photography is contemplated.

*Birds at Bait*

The provision of food in gardens to attract birds is an obvious form of baiting, but in addition a number of birds of the open countryside may be enticed into camera range by the use of suitable baits. The magpie is a good example. Here is a bird very difficult to show at the nest on account of its timidity and cunning, and the often awkward placing of the nest itself. But magpies are omnivorous creatures and are nowadays very common in most agricultural areas where there are high hedges and thickets of thorns. They are readily attracted to suitable baits, especially in the winter.

To outwit them a suitable situation for placing a hide must first be found, preferably in a sheltered spot favourably positioned in respect to the winter sunlight, and in an area frequented by the birds. The hide must be put up some weeks beforehand, and at a suitable distance from it a bait is put down at more or less regular intervals—say every four days. A suitable bait for magpies and such-like carrion feeders consists of a dead rabbit, or a rabbit skin containing offal, and this must be staked down so that the birds cannot drag it away. A dummy lens is used in the usual manner.

The magpies will gradually associate the baiting place with food and will become accustomed to the hide. A fresh bait is laid down when the time comes for the first session. A long wait is likely and two or more people should be available to walk away after the camera has been set up and focused, for magpies are able to count. Ensure that the peg to which the bait is fixed does not show on the screen, and bear in mind that hides do not keep out the cold wind—adequate clothing should be worn. Eric Hosking's idea is to use an old sleeping bag into which the feet are placed and which is drawn up to the waist—a hot-water bottle being put in the bottom if necessary.

A similar baiting procedure may be used to attract other birds that feed on carrion in districts where they are found.

If you have a good working knowledge of bird behaviour other forms of bait will suggest themselves. Thus hips and haws collected from the hedgerows and set up before a hide have been used to attract thrushes and blackbirds to the camera. Successful photographs of that wild winter visitor, the fieldfare, have been obtained in this way, and the idea might be extended to enable starlings to be shown among the elderberries on which they feast so gluttonously in the autumn. Thrushes and blackbirds also respond to fruit windfalls; most of these are collected and a continuous supply maintained in front of the hide. Many finches hang around stack yards in autumn and winter picking up the seeds they find

OUT OF THE BREEDING SEASON. In winter birds of many kinds can be attracted to a bird table and readily photographed from the comfort of the house or garden shed (1). If a natural-looking perch is placed above the table photographs can be obtained without showing the table itself. An attraction for some birds, such as titmice, is a post drilled around the top with holes which are then filled with fat (2). "Wait and see" photography of birds of the estuaries and creeks requires a hide of some kind and a camera with a very long-focus lens (3). Bait can be put down at a hide for some birds, particularly carrion eaters; for these the bait, such as a rabbit, is staked in position so that it cannot be carried off (4).

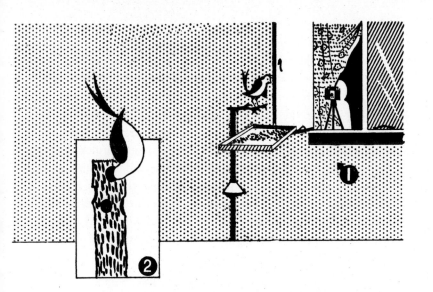

there, and a hide set up in some out-of-the-way corner might prove an excellent means of showing these birds away from the nest. Weed seeds can also be obtained from farmers at threshing time and they form first-rate attractions for many kinds of birds.

Water is a good bait, and although some birds do not drink most of them bathe. The site should be chosen carefully and a small artificial pool about two feet across is made, preferably from concrete. It should be irregular in shape and the surrounding vegetation should be permitted to fall over the sides so that its artificial nature is concealed. Although much can be done beside such a pool, it is in summer when the land is parched and other drinking supplies are drying up that the greatest opportunities are offered.

### Stalking Birds

A bird's senses are so acute and its fear of us so great that it is usually impossible to get close enough by stalking, even with a camera carrying a telephoto lens. But there are some situations in which stalking can succeed. For instance, when woodcock are incubating they often tolerate a close enough approach for photographs to be taken without a hide. Owls roosting in trees will also allow you to get quite close if care is taken to move slowly and indirectly. Then there are the waders which rest in the autumn by muddy streams, sewage farms, and quiet beaches on their way south. Fresh from the Arctic, they have probably had no previous contact with Man and for a while are remarkably tame.

In stalking an individual bird it is advisable not to look directly at it and, if possible, all movement should be gradual and oblique; you should approach circumspectly, for sudden movements are fatal. Stalking is effective among breeding colonies of some seabirds, for many of these—puffins, razorbills, kittiwakes and gannets—are not worried by a cautious approach. In these places the camera may be carried with the tripod attached and ready for action. When close enough to the bird the tripod is set down and the picture taken. A single-lens reflex with a long focus lens or a telephoto is very convenient for this sort of work.

RING-NECKED DUCK. Many species of duck and waterfowl become semi-tame and contentedly live and breed in close proximity to humans on ornamental lakes and pools, even in the cities. They can be readily photographed with a hand-held camera. The ring-necked duck is an American bird.—*Photo*: A. D. Cruickshank.

BIRDS IN THE GARDEN. In winter many kinds of birds can be attracted by a suitably stocked bird table in the garden. A branch or stake should be provided as a "natural" perch. The birds shown are a chaffinch (*top, left*), great tit (*top, right*), long-tailed tit (*bottom, left*) and robin (*bottom, right*).—*Photos:* John Warham. The blue tit (*opposite*) is an entertaining acrobat and likes fat and nuts. Speedflash can be used to prevent blur due to the bird's rapid movements.—*Photo:* John Markham.

BIRDS IN NATURAL HABITAT. In many ways pictures of birds in their natural surroundings can be more attractive than formal poses on a perch. Opportunities often occur when covering a nest from a hide. Robin feeding (*top, left*) and blue tits feeding (*opposite*).—*Photos*: A. Faulkner Taylor. Robin singing (*top, right*), chaffinch and blossom (*bottom, left*) and willow tit (*bottom, right*).—*Photos*: John Markham.

BIRDS IN THE OPEN. Seabirds in their nesting colonies can usually be approached to within fairly close range and photographed from available cover. Otherwise the procedure for birds in the open is to first find cover near a spot likely to be visited and then await events. Razorbill (*top, left*) and puffin (*top, right*).—*Photos:* John Warham. Redshank (*bottom, left*) and yellow-hammer (*bottom, right*).—*Photos:* Eric Hosking. Thick-billed nutcracker, photographed in Sweden (*opposite*).—*Photo:* P. O. Swanberg.

WAIT-AND-SEE. Estuaries are good sites for wait-and-see photography of wild-fowl and waders. A hide is erected and a powerful telephoto lens used on the camera. This picture of a pair of shelduck was obtained at 45 yards range using a 36-in. lens.—*Photo:* A. Faulkner Taylor.


DIPPER (*opposite*). This bird of the mountain streams is a trying subject because it continuously bobs up and down when perched. It has its favourite perching spots whilst feeding, usually on rocks in mid-stream, and the camera can be ranged on one of them in anticipation of a visit.—*Photo:* Harold R. Lowes.

FLIGHT. Gulls are wonderful aerial performers and good subjects for flight pictures. Out of the breeding season they frequent sea fronts, harbours and rivers and can easily be brought within close range

114

of the camera by offerings of titbits. These pictures were obtained by using the top speed of a between-lens shutter and speedflash.—*Photos*: Lindroos.

AMERICAN EGRET. Normally a soft frontal lighting is advised for bird pictures, but given a suitable subject stronger lighting effects—even back lighting, as here—can produce striking pictorial results. This is a wait-and-see picture taken with a 17 in. lens on a 5 × 4 in. camera.—*Photo:* Allan D. Cruickshank.

## Birds on the Wing

During the winter it is good fun attempting pictures of birds in flight. Those which feed in flocks, like gulls, lapwings, and wild-fowl, offer perhaps the greatest opportunities at this time of the year. Once the places to which the birds resort when resting or feeding have been found, the chief problems are how to get near enough and how to tell when they are in focus.

The first is resolved by a study of the lie of the land and a know-ledge of the habits of the birds concerned. It is usually possible to find somewhere to stand, sit or crouch concealed from the birds until they are within range whilst a companion drives them forward. It should be remembered that the birds always rise into the wind, though they will often turn as soon as they are air-borne. So by taking up his stand upwind of the birds the photo-grapher may experience the pleasure of having his quarry fly overhead.

The focusing problem may be tackled in three ways, but in all of them it is desirable to decide beforehand at what distance the pictures are to be taken. The moment when they have reached this distance is gauged, by means of a rangefinder, by the appearance of the image on the ground-glass screen of a reflex camera, or by estimation, the subject being viewed through a wire frame or similar finder and the shutter tripped when the birds are judged to be at the correct distance.

A rangefinder comes into its own when the birds are moving relatively slowly and when it is not desired to take them very close to the camera. They are watched through the rangefinder as they approach and the release is pressed just as the images merge to-gether; the camera is swung of course to follow the birds. For this method the miniature with coupled rangefinder and a long-focus lens is ideal; the focal-plane shutter enables very fast ex-posures and the camera is very compact. The coupled-rangefinder press-type camera would serve equally well. Rangefinders can also be fitted to other cameras and these used in the same way. For example, a single-lens reflex with the focusing hood closed has a rangefinder clipped on top so that the camera can be used at eye level, the lens and rangefinder having previously been set to the same distance.

In the second method the birds are watched on the screen of a reflex and when about to become sharp the shutter is released. Some workers turn out very fine results in this way, though the author has never had much success since it seems difficult to judge just when the birds are sharp; also fast moving objects are difficult to follow on the screen. But the idea works well with slow-moving birds such as soaring eagles, storks or pelicans.

The third way, while rather a hit-or-miss system, is capable of excellent results, although the cameraman's skill at judging the distance of the flying birds is obviously all-important. The advantage of the wire frame type of finder is that it gives an unrestricted view of the whole field, and it is quite easy to see that the birds are central on the negative. In addition the approach of other possible targets may be noted out of the corner of the eye.

When after birds on the wing choose a bright day and go out in the morning or afternoon when the sun is fairly low so that your quarry's flanks and underparts are illuminated as they fly past. On such days a position in the shadow of a bush, or in a dip or ditch where you are not silhouetted, is desirable. It is remarkable how little concealment is needed providing you are seated and motionless, apart from the movement of the camera. Many birds may pass right overhead and will either not see you at all or will be unable to swerve in time. Others may bank away at the last moment, offering a fine opportunity for a shot as they expose their undersides to the sun. Naturally, quite a number of the pictures will be useless because of wing movement or faulty judge-

---

BIRDS IN FLIGHT. Gulls and other sea birds are graceful flyers and are attractive subjects for the camera. A close shot of a bird passing across the line of sight requires the highest shutter speed, such as 1/1000 sec.; but 1/100 sec. is sufficient if the bird approaches head on, and about 1/300 sec. if it approaches at an angle. Lower speeds can be used for more distant shots provided the final picture is intended to show the bird or group of birds as small images against a large area of background. But if it is intended to enlarge a small part of the negative to a great degree to give a "close-up" effect, the highest speed available should still be used; this applies too if a long-focus lens is used to give a larger image.

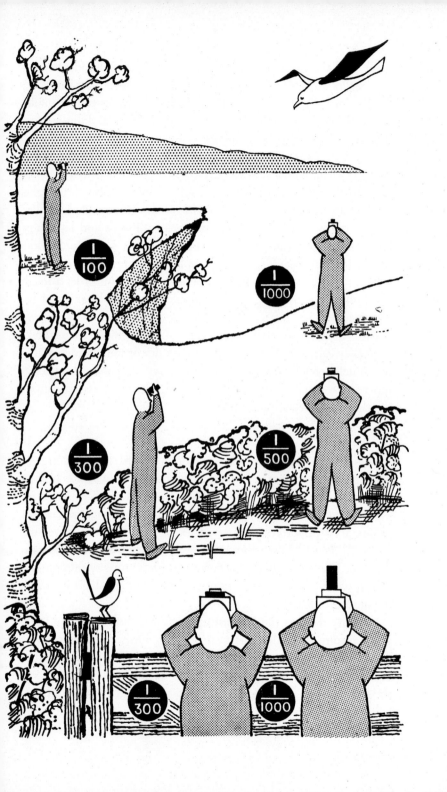

ment, and the more you take the greater the likelihood of first-rate results. Roll films are most convenient to use in plate cameras, for the birds fly over in groups, and unless pictures can be made in rapid succession many chances will be missed. Film packs, though expensive, are even better.

The shutter speeds needed will depend on the speed of the birds, whether their wings beat rapidly or slowly, their distance from the camera and their angle of approach. Gulls may often be caught successfully at 1/250 sec., as may buzzards, vultures and similar birds when soaring on outstretched wings. Rooks and lapwings fairly close to the camera will certainly need 1/500 sec., and wild-fowl with their heavy bodies and rapidly beating wings may take some stopping even at 1/1000 sec. For speeds of this order a focal plane shutter is needed, and this should be correctly adjusted to give true speeds.

Birds directly approaching the camera are the most easily taken, since they can be followed in the viewfinder or rangefinder without much trouble; those passing sideways tend to make tricky shots and a careful swing of the camera must be given to cancel out the birds' forward motion.

### "Wait and See" Photography

Sometimes you cannot help noticing how birds tend to congregate in certain places, or how particular individuals are nearly always flushed from favoured spots—perhaps a patch of sedge in a meadow or part of a filter bed on a sewage farm. Such places are presumably preferred because of the available food, cover or quietness. It may be worth while to put up a hide in such places in the hope of making studies of whatever birds come within range. This is work for the winter months and often the coldest days are the most productive.

In many districts the greatest opportunities for "wait and see" photography lie in the portrayal of water birds on their resting and feeding grounds at lakes and flooded land. The placing of the hide is important. It should enable full advantage to be taken of the sun and be fairly well concealed against a background of bushes or reeds. Naturally it must be put up several weeks before it is likely to be used, and so constructed that gusty winds will not lift the material with which it is covered.

Under these conditions you have to be prepared to take whatever comes within range. It is not practicable to focus on any particular point, and the reflex is used so that as the birds come into view they can be followed and kept in focus up to the moment of exposure. As the camera has to swing from side to side, the slit in the front of the hide through which the lens protrudes must be a horizontal one so that the necessary traversing movements may be made. Even when the birds have been long accustomed to the hide it is not often that they will come close enough for a medium focus lens to be used. A telephoto is a great help but failing this a long-focus lens can be used. Some years ago the author bought a 14-in. $f$5.6 anastigmat and this is fitted to my $3\frac{1}{2} \times 2\frac{1}{2}$ in. reflex by means of an extension box sliding on to the front of the camera. It has proved a profitable investment, and the lens is used either with the focal-plane shutter or with a large sectional one of the Luc pattern fitted behind the lens and operated pneumatically. Such long-focus lenses have only shallow depths of field and they have to be stopped well down. On the other hand with birds afloat an out-of-focus foreground is hardly noticeable.

Working by lakes and flooded land your most likely sitters will be duck, waterhens and herons. Duck may be encouraged near the hide by putting down a little grain from time to time. Duck decoys may also be used; these are floated on the water to one side of the hide and tend to draw down other birds looking for somewhere to alight. On large waters a helper can sometimes edge the birds towards the hide, but if they get too suspicious they are likely to depart for other feeding grounds.

Some bird photographers have produced fine pictures of waders by working in coastal estuaries where there are isolated banks of sand or rock to which the birds retire at high tide. Here they rest to await the ebb and the uncovering of their feeding grounds. As the sea moves in the birds are forced higher and higher until favoured banks above water are covered with waders and gulls of various species. A hide properly placed is usually ignored and many opportunities are given the fortunate occupant.

The "wait and see" method is not likely to commend itself to those who hanker after quick and easy results and it is certainly a time-consuming business, but the photographer's satisfaction at success is all the greater in the knowledge that his pictures have really had to be earned.

# Birds and Flash

CERTAIN BIRDS ARE active at night and must be photographed after dark if their ways are to be recorded. Owls come to mind in this connexion, but there are several other kinds of birds which make nocturnal visits to their nests. The best known are the nightjars and various petrels, the latter comprising a group most of whose members venture ashore only on the darkest of nights. Many other species of birds—herons, nightingales, waders and wildfowl—are active both by day and night, though usually they do not visit their nests after dark.

Bird photography with flash is not difficult and it can certainly be exciting. Much of the fascination lies in not knowing just what the camera has recorded—if anything at all. Early flashlight pictures of animals and birds were taken by means of flash powder, which was either ignited loose in special trays or detonated under compression. Often the subject under fire and the firer were equally scared by the subsequent explosion. The development of the flashbulb gave a great impetus to the use of this type of illumination for nature photography, and interest in flash has been further increased by the advent of electronic flash. Some fine results have been secured by workers both at home and overseas.

## Using Flashbulbs

The only additional equipment needed for the night-time photography of birds with flash is a suitable reflector and bulb-holder connected through a switch to a battery so that the bulb is fired when the switch is closed. The only extra step to be taken in preparing the hide is to include a shiny tin lid to simulate a reflector and accustom the birds to this bright object. Reflectors are conveniently fixed to ball-and-socket heads so that the light can be thrown in any required direction, and they may be fastened to the hide uprights or to any convenient support. It is important to be able to reach the bulbs from within; this means that in practice the reflector or reflectors must be placed close to the lens and a slit made in the fabric to allow the hand ready access when replacing the expended bulb with a new one.

The flash reflectors should be placed higher than the camera and a little to one side so that adequate modelling is obtained. Often only one bulb will be fired at a time but two are easily wired up to fire simultaneously if desired. The flash reflectors must be correctly centred so that the light is thrown squarely on to the subject and a check can be made by placing the head where it is expected the bird will stand. On looking at the reflectors it will readily be seen whether any alteration is needed.

If a systematic arrangement of your gear inside the hide is desirable for daylight working it is essential at night. Things must be so organized that any item can be reached instantly in the dark. Slides must be set out in the correct sequence for using, thermos and food handy, and so on. Check also that the flashbulbs really can be changed from within the hide without difficulty. It is equally essential to have the gear all assembled and the camera focused in daylight. It is possible to focus on a hand-held torch after dark, but this is most inconvenient and undesirable since most nocturnal birds become active at dusk and often offer the best opportunities for pictures at that time. If you are not well settled down before they begin to stir, they may be startled to discover intruders near their nests when they are bringing the first feeds of the night.

### Seeing What Goes On

If you wish to learn something of the birds' behaviour in addition to photographing them, it is obviously necessary to see what is happening at the nest. On moonlight nights and in the early

NIGHTINGALE IN AGGRESSIVE ATTITUDE. Flash can easily result in an under-exposed, or even completely unexposed, background. This is legitimate for nocturnal birds but not for others. The nightingale, although very much a bird of the daytime, is nevertheless noted for his singing into the late hours, so the black background here can pass as authentic.—*Photo:* Eric Hosking.

**HOOPOE WITH FOOD** (*top, left*). This colourful bird occasionally breeds in Britain. It is not nocturnal in habits, so the black background is unnatural. But it is an informative action picture taken by speedflash as the bird flies to its nest hole.— *Photo:* G. Schutzenhofer.

**LITTLE OWL WITH EARTH-WORM** (*top, right*). Owls are nocturnal, so that the use of flash not only gives a natural result but it is necessary to secure any result at all. The bird is flying to its nest hole.— *Photo:* Eric Hosking.

**WREN WITH FLIES** (*left*). Flash in daylight gives natural results if the background is close enough to receive as much light as the bird.—*Photo:* G. Schutzenhofer.

SPOTTED FLYCATCHER FEEDING YOUNG (*top, left*). Speedflash is ideal for feeding pictures, as there is a good deal of subject movement.—*Photo:* Eric Hosking.

HOOPOE FEEDING YOUNG (*top, right*). The tree trunk receives the flash and produces a more natural result than the hoopoe picture on the opposite page.—*Photo:* G. Schutzenhofer.

BARN OWL WITH PREY (*right*). Flashbulbs can be used with fairly static subjects.—*Photo:* John Warham.

127

SWALLOW BRAKING. Speedflash is valuable in the study of bird flight. The bird is checking its momentum as it approaches the nest.—*Photo:* G. Schutzenhofer.

CROSSBILL BRAKING. Not quite as graceful as the swallow opposite, but it adopts a similar technique.—*Photo:* G. Schutzenhofer.

129

MEADOW PIPIT (*opposite, top*). An excellent example of speedflash technique. A backcloth provides a plain background to the bird as it flies off its nest on the ground.—*Photo:* Eric Hosking.

GOLDFINCH FEEDING (*opposite, bottom*). The bird flutters its wings to steady itself on the thistle head.—*Photo:* G. Schutzenhofer.

LITTLE OWL FLYING TO NEST HOLE (*above*). The bird is braking for the landing. —*Photo:* John Warham.

STOCK DOVE ALIGHTING (*right*). The background is rather underexposed, but the effect is not entirely unnatural. —*Photo:* John Warham.

GREAT TIT IN FLIGHT (*opposite*). The head-on view provides a striking and un-usual result, but timing the exposure as the bird comes into focus requires con-siderable skill. The shot was taken with a long-focus lens as the bird approached its nest hole.—*Photo:* G. Schutzenhofer.

LINNET LANDING (*above, and pages* 134, 135). A series of flight study pictures can be readily assembled if the bird makes frequent visits to a particular perch and therefore enables many pictures to be taken.—*Photos:* G. Schutzenhofer.

WOOD THRUSH AT BATH. A striking example of the wait-and-see procedure combined with speedflash. The young fern fronds, catching the flash in addition to the bird and immediate foreground, help in disguising the fact that flash was used as well as enhancing the pictorial appeal of the picture. This is an American bird. —*Photo:* Allan D. Cruickshank.

136

evening this is easy enough, but when dark it may be quite impossible to see anything but the vague shapes of the trees around you. Peering out into the gloom like this is very trying and tiring; trees and branches start to move and it is very annoying after firing a bulb to realize that you have been deceived by a knobbly branch. Furthermore you may fall asleep and miss a feed altogether. This is easily done when owls are the quarry, since these birds wear feathers so designed that they make no sound as they stroke the air with their wings; if the birds do not call before coming in and the young do not advertise their nearness by giving the hunger call, the only indication of the adults' coming may be the rasp of talons on a branch.

Fortunately, although effective under conditions when our own are naturally useless, owls' eyes are not sensitive to the red end of the spectrum and in my experience all the common species will ignore dull red lights. With their aid the nest can be illuminated and the birds' movements observed. The red light must not flicker or move (a battery of adequate capacity is necessary) and the switch should be silent. With the nest lit up in this way it is easy to see when to fire the flash, and if desired another red light can be used inside the hide for note-taking. One pair of barn owls studied some years ago permitted me to use a white light at their nest, and later I even made a cine film of their activities with the aid of two 500-watt floods without causing any alarm. Nightjars would probably accept a red illuminant, and shearwaters and other nocturnal petrels show no fear of red or white lights providing these are neither bright nor flickering.

A companion is needed to see you into the hide in the usual way and a relief is most desirable since nothing is more likely to upset the birds than your sudden emergence from the hide at the end of a session, and it is often impossible to tell whether or not they are in the neighbourhood. However, it will generally be found that there is little activity at an owl's nest after midnight so that you can generally pack up before it gets too late.

The frequency of an owl's visits depends to some extent on the age of the owlets. When these are small the hen bird will spend a lot of time with them, brooding, tearing up the prey brought in by the cock, and so on. Later both bring food to the nest. Sometimes long intervals occur between feeds and on nights which are dark, windy, or wet, little activity will be seen, for under these conditions hunting is difficult and often abortive; so is owl photography.

Summer nights in Britain can be very cold and if you contemplate an all-night session several pairs of socks may be needed and a blanket for use in the small hours of the morning.

Be careful when working with owls, for some kinds—notably the tawny owl of Britain and some of the horned owls overseas—will attack those who approach their nests after dark. A hat should always be worn when working near the nest, or a coat thrown over the head; perhaps even a fencing mask if your particular birds are known to be an aggressive couple, since owls generally strike at the head with their strong talons.

A difficulty encountered when using bulbs at night is that the birds may see your hand as you reach out to remove the spent one; if they do there will be a violent volley of abuse and you may see no more of them for the rest of the night. Allow plenty of time after the bird's departure before trying to effect the change-over. Move the hand very slowly in case the bird is still about or take advantage of its disappearance into the nesting hole to change the bulbs while she is with the chicks. If two reflectors are used one bulb can be fired at a time and two exposures made before a change is needed.

### The Open-Flash Method

At dusk and after dark the ambient light is so low that no fogging of a plate will occur if the shutter is open for several seconds, and pictures may be made using the open-flash technique, the shutter being opened, the bulb fired, and the shutter closed. When it is really dark the shutter can be set in the open position with little danger of anything being recorded unless the skyline is included or the moon comes out.

Flashbulbs take varying times to burn according to the size and make, but even the large ones which allow small stops to be used give a flash duration of about 1/40 sec., and the smaller kinds, which are often quite adequate, are rather faster than this. Thus it is not difficult to get pictures free from movement. Owls in particular perch readily and often sit quite motionless, making the "open-flash" method quite feasible. If the bird holds a rodent in its beak the bulb should not be fired until the animal's tail has ceased to swing, otherwise your picture may be marred by the blur of the prey.

It will be found that owls soon become accustomed to sudden flashes; at first they may fly off, but usually they hold their ground and probably turn to glower in the direction of the hide. If you have two reflectors you may be able to get a second shot as the bird stares straight at the lens, providing you can change plates or wind on the film quickly enough. When visits are infrequent this arrangement, which enables two pictures to be made in quick succession, is a great help, and if two cameras are used there is no need to change over plates. Another advantage given by two bulbs operated separately is that you can choose which to fire according to whether the bird faces to the left or right. The point here is that the light should be so arranged that the shadow of the head is thrown behind the body. Otherwise the bird's profile tends to be lost among the shadow. If the bird is looking to your left the left-hand bulb should be fired and *vice versa*; if full face, then either will do.

The stop needed will vary with the size of the bulb. The maker's recommendations are used until your trials have established the correct guide number for your particular materials, development technique and other conditions.

## The Synchronized Shutter

Although the open-flash method is cheap and effective, the fact that before darkness sets in the shutter must be opened before the flash is fired calls for some concentration. The birds will often arrive unexpectedly, and it is easy in the excitement of the moment to do the wrong thing—to fire the bulb with the shutter still closed. For this and other reasons it is easier if the switch firing the flash is incorporated in the shutter so that when this is opened the current flows to the bulb. You can then concentrate on taking the photograph at the correct moment rather than on purely mechanical details.

Luc-type shutters are easily synchronized for flashbulbs, internal contacts being fitted by any repair firm so that the peak of the flash takes place when the blades are fully open. Modern shutters are already synchronized.

Synchronization is of two types, M and X. M-synchronization involves a timing mechanism in the shutter so as to delay its opening for about 1/50 sec. after electrical contact has been made. This is necessary for all flashbulbs (except the Speed Midget) if synchronization is required at all shutter speeds. With X-synchronization contact is made when the shutter is fully open. This is essential for electronic flash, and is satisfactory for flashbulbs up to a shutter speed of 1/50 sec.

Modern Prontor, Compur and focal-plane shutters (on precision miniatures) are M and X-synchronized. If old shutters are fitted with synchronizing contacts this will have to be X-type, but this will meet the bird photographer's requirements since it is normal to use electronic flash for speed work, and not flashbulbs.

*Electronic Flash*

Flashbulbs have a number of disadvantages in operation. The bulbs are expendable which makes much work rather expensive, and there is the inevitable delay between exposures while the bulbs are changed over, a procedure that may not be easy with nervous sitters. And the flash is seldom short enough to give sharp pictures if the bird is moving.

In recent years electronic flash has become a commonplace tool for amateur and professional photographers in all fields of work. The light emitted by the tube is brilliant, of short duration, similar to daylight in colour and of soft contrast. The tube is not expendable but capable of giving many thousands of flashes. Such properties are of great value to the bird photographer.

The high-speed flash unit used by the author has a total power output of 200 joules when two lamps are used. This is adequate for most ornithological occasions when working with black-and-white materials. Even so the weight of the gear is about 18 lb. so that a price has to be paid for the benefits conferred by this type of lighting.

When much flash has to be used the electronic method scores hands down over bulbs on the cost factor. There is a high initial cost for the outfit, but each tube should give 10,000 flashes before its life is done, so that the cost per flash works out very cheaply in the long run.

The circuits used are not really complicated and a capable radio engineer would have no difficulty in constructing one given the necessary diagram. When the equipment first came on the market there was something to be said for having it built privately, but nowadays with prices lower and reliability higher, there is little advantage in home construction.

As with consumable bulbs the open-flash method may be used with electronic flash when taking birds after dark, but to employ it only under such circumstances would be to limit severely its scope and possibilities, for this type of lighting can be used as effectively in daylight as at night-time. Open flash cannot be used in daylight since the ambient light is too great and duplicate images will be obtained; to avoid this it is necessary to use an X-synchronized shutter.

In use the shutter may be set to any desired speed since the flash duration is so short (about 1/3000 sec.) that it cannot overlap the shutter's opening. Thus with a silent type shutter used at top speed the blades open for about 1/40 sec. in the middle of which the flash falls for 1/3000 sec.; likewise with a Compur at 1/400 sec. the flash takes place in the middle of this brief opening of the leaves. Focal plane shutters are not suitable except at a low speed (usually 1/20–1/30 sec.) when the slit is fully open, otherwise only that portion of the film opposite the slit will show an image on development.

It should be noted that flash units employing low voltage

electrolytic capacitors give a rather lower flash-speed than that stated—about 1/800–1/1000 sec.

## The Speedlamp in the Field

The setting up of the camera and the high-speed gear in a hide involves no great changes from normal flash procedure. The birds should be inured to the reflectors as usual by setting up suitable dummies in advance, and inside the hide the power unit and its switches must be conveniently placed by the left hand so that the other is free to operate the antinous release—that is, assuming you are right-handed. Since it is no longer necessary to change bulbs after each exposure, the reflectors can be placed out of reach of the hand and there is no need to make a slit in the canvas as when working with bulbs. For this reason it is best to mount the reflectors on stands of some sort—the telescopic portable variety used for carrying photofloods in studios and elsewhere are excellent, and the tripod-type legs can be forced into the ground to give additional stability. Light-weight photographic tripods can be used similarly, ball-and-socket heads enabling the reflectors to be readily adjusted to any desired position.

In most cases power will be derived from batteries; an accumulator is normally used and can be recharged at home from an inexpensive trickle charger. The flash unit must be kept charged so that it can be flashed instantly when required. This means that it may have to be kept switched on for most of the time. If they are not fully charged when the bird arrives and the release is pressed, then either no flash is forthcoming or the light emitted may be below normal in output and an under-exposed negative will result. Where the photographer has plenty of notice of the old birds' approach it will not be necessary for the tubes to be ready

---

FLASH. A convenient way to set up electronic flash is to mount it on a tripod with a ball-and-socket head, or on a camera clamp fixed to a stake or the hide framework (1). The set-up shows an outfit and extension set coupled to fire together. Flash bulbs can be used, particularly for nocturnal birds; but bulb changing is a disadvantage, and if the subject is a tawny owl the photographer should at least wear eye protection lest he is attacked (2). Electronic flash is valuable for birds in flight; a simple set-up is to arrange a baited perch against a background cloth and shoot on the hit or miss principle as the birds come and go.

for immediate use, but often such a warning is not given. Most units have a small neon lamp which glows when the minimum voltage has been built up; this is a big help in the dark.

Sets incorporating a vibrator emit a humming sound when switched on; birds generally show no alarm at this, for it is a steady noise and not usually loud. With ground-nesting kinds I prefer to raise the power unit off the floor of the hide, hanging it by a nail from a hide pole or standing it on a wad of canvas, so that vibration and noise are not carried through the ground to scare the bird: possibly an unnecessary precaution.

With electronic flash all normal movement of the subject is eliminated, the action being arrested as the bird is momentarily illuminated. Thus there is no excuse for lack of crispness since, providing the camera has been correctly positioned and the bird is in focus, it will be rendered with detail as fine as the lens can produce. There can be no such thing as camera shake when working with electronic flash. It becomes unnecessary to wait until the bird is motionless before exposing; indeed, action is desirable. Thus the eager upturned beaks of young chicks can be caught with beautiful precision without the usual irritating blur resulting. For all this the release must not be pressed blindly. It is still important to judge the correct moment for taking the picture. This time, however, you are not looking for a chance to slip in an exposure while the bird is still, but simply ensuring that it will be shown in a pleasing and natural posture or to catch an interesting episode.

Again, as with ordinary daylight photography, rear views and full-face shots are seldom satisfactory and it is important to try to catch the bird when the eye can be seen. A good highlight in the eye is a great asset in a bird photograph and almost certain to be obtained with flash. Wait for the right moment (but don't wait too long), anticipate the bird's next move and press the release accordingly; if your focusing was right then the record should be a true one.

Two lamps can be used as easily as one, the leads from each being plugged to a single lead to the shutter by a double connector. Another method finding favour these days is to fire the second (or even a third) tube photo-electrically, the light from the main lamp triggering off the "slave" lamps. The greater the number of flash heads the longer the effective flash duration.

*Owls and the Speedlamp*

Owing to the short duration of the flash, which is over and done with before they have time to move, owls and other birds of nocturnal habits seldom take exception to speedlamp photography. The flash temporarily blinds them though, if they are looking directly at the reflectors when the tube is fired, and should they be in flight then they are likely to crash into obstructions during their blackout. The photographer who makes the birds his first consideration will avoid this. Owls make fascinating subjects for electronic flash photography, especially when the young are old enough to come to the entrance of the nesting hole at meal times, or in situations where the camera can see right into the nest—as may be possible with barn owls in pigeon cotes and lofts, or with tawny and long-eared owls in the old nests of other birds.

*The Speedlamp in Daylight*

One of the snags encountered when using electronic flash by day is the lack of penetration into the background, so that while the main object may be adequately lit the background is underexposed and comes out dark in the print. Thus a bird perched on a post in the sun and pictured with the speedlamp at a shutter setting of, say, 1/200 sec. is illuminated solely by the flash when the stop is *f*16 or smaller. Little or no daylight will register on the film and the bird will be shown against a very dark or completely black background. This is undesirable because it is unnatural—the bird is not a nocturnal one.

What can be done to avoid such false renderings? In the first place the situation in which the pictures are to be made must be carefully chosen. The nest sites most suited for speed-gun photography are those with fairly close backgrounds or those situated in crevices on tree trunks, in ivy against walls, in banks and suchlike spots. And although the nest should have a background it is better if this is not too close, for if it is not out of focus the bird may be lost against it. Great depth of focus is by no means always an asset in bird work.

There are times when an otherwise unsuitable site may be taken against a backcloth, but this is a procedure only possible with the tamest of species, with titmice and garden birds for instance. A backcloth if used must be light in colour to be effective—pale green is as good a shade as any—and if possible it should be fixed little more than two feet behind the nest. It is important to see that the material is quite tight and does not sag on its supports as folds will be very obvious in a print. Probably a painted sheet of plywood or hardboard would be ideal for the purpose. Needless to say any backcloth introduced to a nesting site has to be set up in stages if the birds are not to be alarmed.

Another way in which black backgrounds may be avoided is to use comparatively slow shutter speeds so that both daylight and flash are recorded. A guide here is to set the shutter speed for the background and the iris for the flash. For example, suppose the flash requires an aperture of $f16$, an exposure reading of the background is taken and the shutter speed noted for an aperture of $f16$. If this is, say, 1/100 sec. then a camera setting of 1/100 sec. and $f16$ will provide a correctly exposed background, and the flash will fully illuminate the subject. If the natural lighting on the subject is as bright as that on the background this might result in over-exposure of the subject. The best course is then to reckon the aperture required by the flash as one stop smaller than it would normally require—in this case $f22$. The camera would then be set at 1/50 sec. and $f22$; this gives the same exposure to the background as 1/100 sec. and $f16$, but the smaller stop reduces the effect of the flash on the subject. If this is still too bright in the picture the process can be continued to 1/25 sec. and $f32$, and so on.

The obvious snag with such a method is that an important advantage of electronic flash—its speed and consequent elimination of failures due to subject movement— is relinquished, for if the bird moves during the period that the shutter is open, the daylight image will show movement and the negative will be a jumble with one image imperfectly superimposed on the other. All the same, when you are not concerned with getting action pictures the method has much to commend it, and a few experiments with various kinds of subject will establish the best relationship between stop and shutter speed when using daylight and flash together.

The tendency to get inadequate lighting of the background is aggravated if the reflector is placed too low. Ideally, to ensure that the foreground and the background of a nest are equally illuminated, the flash head should be vertically above it throwing the light straight down. Such an arrangement is obviously undesirable and impracticable, so a compromise has to be made, the lamp or lamps being fixed well above the level of the camera and probably some feet forward of it. Even with this set-up, however, the foreground will get a greater amount of light than the rest of the picture. How to deal with this when printing is discussed later in this chapter.

### The Speedlamp and Bird Flight

Although a number of nature photographers using cameras with specially speeded shutters had made quite effective pictures of birds on the wing at close quarters, not until the advent of electronic flash was the portrayal of small birds in flight really a feasible proposition for most of us. The light from the flash-tube is normally quite short enough to arrest wing movement and to record feather detail; but where small, fast-moving birds like tits and wrens are concerned, it is difficult to eliminate movement completely, especially in certain parts of the wing stroke. Such movement is seldom serious enough to mar the results if focusing has been carried out correctly, only the wing tips being blurred a little. With low capacity, high voltage condensers the shorter the leads from lamps to power and extension units, the more rapid the flash given; if you require the greatest speed from your unit this should be borne in mind.

Outfits working at high voltages and having low capacity condensers are of the type which have been discussed so far and are characterized by the short flash duration—generally of the order of 1/3000 sec. Another type, introduced in a successful bid to reduce weight, use high capacity electrolytic condensers at low voltages. They employ the "hairpin" form of flash-tube as opposed to the spiral ones of the previous type. These low voltage sets have some advantages apart from their lower weight, but for the photographer wishing to show birds on the wing they are unsuitable since the flash duration is comparatively long (1/800 to 1/1000 sec.) and inadequate to freeze wing movement, though fast enough for many other phases of bird work.

When taking birds on the wing at close quarters it is a big help if the subject can be caught on a known line of flight. For this reason most pictures of this kind are made as the bird flies from a perch to a given point (the nest or food) or as it leaves such places.

In setting up the camera for shots of this kind a piece of string fastened from the perch to the nest, or a thin stick laid across, is useful in indicating the expected path of movement of the bird and to act as your focusing guide. The bird's customary line of approach will have been ascertained by prior observation. In this way you can adjust the camera with reasonable accuracy so that a definite section of the path of movement is covered. The guide should not be arranged to coincide with the path of the bird's body, but placed a little forward of this to come about two-thirds along the nearer wing when this is at the centre of the down beat. On stopping down the band of sharp focus will then include the wing nearest the camera, the bird's body and possibly most of the far wing as well. If the line of flight is not exactly parallel with the plate, the side swing of the camera back is brought into play to make the focal plane coincide with the flight path.

Often the distance between perch and alighting point will be no greater than six feet, but of course the lens will probably cover only a part of this distance, unless the hide is placed right back. When taking the photographs you have to make sure that the bird is in the appropriate section of the flight path at the moment of exposure; frequently objects in the background can be used to gauge this correctly. As soon as the bird leaves its perch the fingers must be ready to press the release. Judgement of the correct moment is not easy; often you are too late, but skill comes with practice. It is particularly exasperating to discover on development that the bird's head is just coming into the picture, or its tail vanishing across the edge of the negative. Not long ago I had the chance of getting a shot of a rare Australian bird never previously photographed; as it flew from its roosting hole the flash was fired but my judgement was faulty and all that the negative showed was the end of an exquisitely sharp tail. Such disappointments come the way of all of us and our initial failures pave the way for eventual success.

Triggering of the tubes can be done electrically by means of the device upon which many burglar alarms are based. The method is to project a narrow beam of light (visible or infra-red) across the flight path of the bird and directed at a photoelectric cell. This operates a relay which holds in the open position a switch in the flash circuit as long as the beam falls on the cell and generates current. Immediately the beam is cut by the bird passing through it the switch closes and the flash fires. Such devices are out of reach of many of us, and perhaps this may be all to the good for they would seem to remove much of the skill otherwise necessary and with it the satisfaction gained from doing the work unaided. At the same time close-range flight pictures are very much hit-and-miss whatever skill is applied, and these devices lead to a greater measure of certainty.

For flying shots by day a shutter speed must be used that is fast enough to prevent the recording of any daylight image. In the absence of an adequate background the pictures will, of course, appear to have been taken at night; a careful choice of site and the correct camera angle are once again important if this is to be avoided. With small birds at the feeding table or elsewhere in the garden a backcloth will prove useful. Should the distance include any brightly-lit areas, such as blobs of sky filtering between branches, or patches of light foliage bathed in sunlight, then particular care will be needed. Otherwise you may find a patch of sky registering "through" the bird's wing: in the time that elapses between the shutter's opening and the flash, the sky may record on the emulsion after which the bird's motion carries it forward until the wing comes in line with the light patch and in this position is recorded by the flash. For such situations a synchronized Luc is not suitable; at least 1/200 sec. is needed and this is most conveniently given with a speeded sectional shutter of the Compound, Compur or Prontor type.

A bird in flight presents a much larger object than it does when at rest. Accordingly a lens-to-subject distance suitable for the usual stationary pictures will be too great for convenience when making flight studies. Either the hide must be moved farther back or a lens of shorter focal length used. It is important not to be too close when attempting flight shots, not only because of the shallow depth of field that results (though this is somewhat modified by the smaller stops used) but also because the closer the camera the more difficult it is to judge the correct moment for firing the flash and the greater the number of rejects that are secured. My own method is to take static subjects with an 8 in. lens and switch to a 6½ in. one for the occasional flight picture needed to complete a series.

### The Speedlamp in the Rain

Commercially designed outfits are not intended to be used outdoors in wet or damp weather. Unfortunately the bird-worker cannot be sure when he has set up his gear that the weather will remain fine for the rest of the session. Should rain begin to fall he may be unable to leave his post for fear of putting off the bird, and chicks and eggs soon come to grief in heavy rain. At the same time he may be unable to take any pictures because of the danger that water may cause a short circuit or even a serious electrical breakdown. The high voltages set up in the power unit are great enough to be dangerous to the user, and special care is taken in their design to ensure adequate insulation. With such high charges it would be crazy to operate in wet weather without taking special precautions.

Speedlamps can, however, be weather-proofed. The main difficulty is the flash head, for this is outside the hide and fully exposed to the elements. It is necessary to seal the base of the tube so that no water can possibly get down into the socket. This can be done with the help of a suitable plastic insulating compound or by the provision of a sleeve of thin rubber (such as a portion of a toy balloon) which is pulled over the base of the tube and on to the top of the holder. Sealing the power unit inside the hide is not so difficult. It should be raised off the ground so that water cannot seep in underneath and can be completely covered with a piece of rubberized fabric in the event of stray drops getting in through peepholes or from the roof. See that water cannot run down the lamp leads to the plugs on the main or extension units. Another point to insulate properly is the connexion between the synchro-lead and the flash head and the camera shutter must also be protected from rain-drops—a waterproof cloth draped over the camera will be sufficient. These precautions will usually enable you to carry on through light showers, but in the event of heavy rain the unit should be disconnected and everything dried out before re-use. If in doubt whether it is safe to use the speedgun, don't!

When there is a lot of humidity in the air, even though rain may not be falling, there is frequently a diminution of the light output —no doubt power seeps away unused under these conditions. Reflectors readily become misted up in damp weather and may cease to reflect efficiently; the trouble may also be encountered when the hide is placed over water and can be cured by rubbing the reflectors over with glycerin.

*Exposure, Development and Enlarging*

The stop needed when working with electronic flash is readily obtained once the "flash factor" of the unit has been determined. This is a multiple of the lamp-to-subject distance and the stop, so that the stop is obtained by dividing the flash number by the distance in feet. The factor varies with the speed of the photographic material used. Note that published speeds of films and plates may have little relevance when you are using electronic flash; a film rated faster than another of the same manufacture to daylight or to tungsten lamps, may be found slower in comparison when electronic flash is the illuminant. The flash factor is thus best found by trial and error.

As a guide, a 100-joule outfit may be expected to have a factor of at least 100 with high-speed pan. film. This implies that a correctly exposed negative will be obtained at $f20$ when lamp-to-subject is five feet ($100 \div 5 = 20$), or $f10$ at ten feet, and so on. The flash factor known, it is only necessary to measure with a tape the distance from lens to nest and to divide this distance in feet into the flash factor; the result is the stop required. Where two 100-joule tubes are employed the flash factor will be in the region of 150 for high-speed emulsions.

Electronic flash gives images showing rather soft contrasts and it is customary to lengthen development times by about 50 per cent to offset this; the author's preference is to give about 25 per cent extra development to get negatives slightly on the soft side but full of detail. Any standard developer may be used. Once a suitable technique has been worked out to give you the sort of negatives you like, changes should not be made unless real advantages are going to result.

When enlarging, some control will be helpful in correcting over-lit foregrounds, such as by progressively shading the projected image from the top downwards. Apart from over-all shading such as this, it will often be found necessary to hold back parts of the background and to print out the fronts of nests, tree trunks and so on to achieve an improved and balanced picture.

### The Potentialities of Electronic Flash

Apart from its obvious application to the study of the flight of birds, the speed-lamp is proving of great value to the serious bird-photographer and to the ornithologist who wishes to portray those fleeting and ephemeral aspects of bird behaviour so often impossible to record except at high speeds. With its aid it has been possible to make accurate records of experiments upon enemy recognition in birds, to make pictures having such clarity of detail that insects being fed to the young can be readily identified, and to show a wide variety of incidents which otherwise could never have been attempted. The field for further exploitation of electronic flash and the possibilities of doing original and valuable work are great.

It is not only the speed of the flash which is so valuable, but also the constancy of the light and its close approximation to daylight in quality. For these reasons electronic flash is very suitable for use with colour film, although as these are rather slower than black-and-white, even a 200-joule unit is not powerful enough unless quite large apertures are used. Such a unit would have some possibilities in conjunction with a miniature camera for the making of colour pictures suitable for projection, since a large stop is not such a disadvantage on 35 mm. film where the comparatively short-focus lenses give good depths of field. Larger units are heavier and not really practicable and they are more expensive. High-powered units are made for studio use, but these are mains operated and so unsuited for field work.

The ideal equipment for a bird photographer would seem to be one giving a light-output of about 800 joules at a flash duration of not greater than 1/5000 sec., this light being split between two lamps and the whole outfit being really portable. The condensers should be able to retain their charge over long periods and the whole thing should be shower proof. Such a unit would enable all phases of bird behaviour to be shown in full colour; for black-and-white photography either a lower light output could be used or slower and finer-grained emulsions employed. As it is, flash-bulbs have to be used for this kind of work, and they are more expensive, less convenient in use and are not suitable for high-speed shots.

# In the Tropics

THE TROPICAL REGIONS of the world are well known for their wealth of animal life and for the colourful and even bizarre varieties of birds to be found there. Endless opportunities exist for bird photography, and although much fine work has been done in the warmer parts of the world and in the southern hemisphere, many species have yet to be photographed and many more have only been pictured quite inadequately.

The conditions under which bird photography is undertaken in tropical areas may be very different from those prevailing in Europe or Britain. Heat, humidity, and dust raise problems, as does the frequent shortage of water suitable for processing. Bad communications are often a bugbear. The weather is often predictable with cloudless skies day after day, while the rains may fall at more or less regular seasons during which movement of vehicles may be impossible. Breeding seasons generally follow the rains, though many sea-birds nest all the year round. The general methods of using hides as described in previous pages still apply and it is surprising how timid many kinds of land birds prove to be in remote areas where human beings are seldom seen.

## Nesting Birds

The tropics are noted for the large colonies of sea-birds—sometimes numbering a million or more individuals—which resort to isolated islands for nesting. Such places offer wonderful opportunities for photography. The birds may be very tame. I have walked through colonies of noddy terns where the nests were so thick on the ground that one had to step over the sitting birds, most of which refused to leave their eggs, merely raising their beaks and wings in aggressive display. But while it is unnecessary to use hides with such fearless individuals, I always prefer to work concealed when time allows. This ensures that your subjects act naturally, will carry on with their domestic duties—feeding the chicks, flirting with their mates, bickering with their neighbours —without being distracted and angered by your movements.

The enormous numbers of birds in such colonies may raise special problems. One of these is how to isolate individual pairs for photography. Although you may wish to show something of the colony as a whole and to include many nests on one negative, for close-up work it is better to concentrate on a single nest. And it may be difficult to find one where the heads or tails of neighbours do not intrude distractingly into the picture area. The thing to do is to search around the edges of the colony where isolated pairs are more frequent. If the hide can be sited to overlook several nests some feet apart, then it is possible by swinging the camera to get photographs of each (perhaps at different stages of the breeding cycle) during a single session. With tame birds of this kind it is sufficient to fix up the hide without any preliminaries, but it is generally best to leave it in position for a day or so beforehand. Even with isolated nests it will be found that off-duty birds frequently walk into the picture area to sleep or preen just where they are out of focus and unwanted, but that is all part of the game and only to be expected in such crowded communities.

The huge clouds of birds hovering over their breeding grounds are well worth recording, but your efforts to do this may be foiled time and again by a knot of inquisitive or aggressive individuals which hang calling in the air above; some of these generally succeed in getting into the picture, and being far too close to the camera spoil shot after shot. And where such numbers are encountered camera and cameraman inevitably get spattered with droppings.

A tremendous amount of light is reflected from the sand and coral beaches typical of many tropical sea-bird colonies and small stops and short exposures are possible. Situations tend to be

contrasty, but good negatives for enlarging can usually be produced without the need for a flash fill-in if you over-expose and
curtail development.

### Baiting in the Tropics

Two forms of bait are particularly effective in hot climates—
carrion and water.

Carrion in the form of carcases, entrails, waste food and so on,
forms a powerful attraction for birds like kites, vultures, many
kinds of eagles and sea eagles, and to crows and magpies. The hide,
for obvious reasons, should be pitched up-wind and well away
from the bait (a telephoto lens comes into its own here) and should
be set up days or weeks before photography begins. If a perch can
be provided on to which incoming birds can alight before dropping down to feed, so much the better.

Water exerts a powerful attraction to birds of many kinds, the
more so during dry seasons and periods of drought. Advantage
can be taken of drying up water holes in the beds of rivers and
elsewhere to site a hide and record the various visitors that come
down to drink. The photographer can also provide a water-bait
in the shape of an artificial pool, and the best method is to arrange
for the water to drip down from a can set up in a nearby bush. A
hose fitted with a tap is used to control the flow of water drop by
drop. Dripping water is very effective and the cameraman carefully concealed will have no shortage of subjects.

### Swamps, Deserts and Forests

Bird life is often prolific around tropical swamps and lakes and
methods of finding nests follow the same patterns as in more
temperate regions. Mosquitoes are usually bad and so are the snakes.
An inflatable rubber dinghy is very handy for searching around
the edges of the water. Even though lakes are shallow enough for
wading, the dinghy can be used for carrying gear to and from
hides placed in trees or on islands rising from the water.

In semi-desert areas thorny scrub is widespread and even this arid country may carry quite a heavy stock of breeding birds following the rains. The bushes may grow up to thirty feet or so, but generally without a straight branch in them and little suitable for hide making. Yet at times nests may be everywhere among the scrub—eagles and hawks in the bigger bushes and other birds lower down. Long hide poles have to be included in the equipment if it is intended to tackle the higher nests in this type of country.

On the sand plains, especially where the vegetation is sparse, it is a sensible precaution to fit an optical flat into the filter holder in front of the lens to protect it from the scouring action of wind-blown sand. The same device will prevent salt spray getting to the lens surfaces when the camera is used by the sea. When sand blows it is difficult to keep cameras and equipment clean, but this must be done somehow or much damage may result and films may be ruined through abrasion marks and "tram-lines".

In the forests and timbered country the common problem is the excessive contrasts encountered owing to the patches of light that filter down through the trees. Even among scrub, nests and their surroundings are inclined to be very contrasty and much tropical bird photography suffers from excessive "soot and whitewash". This problem is easily solved by the consistent use of flash fill-in, and the rule given earlier "stop for the flash, shutter speed for the background", again applies. Since the sun is generally high in the sky, reflectors will be placed at camera level.

I find a satisfactory arrangement is to have two lamps, only one of which is used at a time. With the hide placed north of the nest (in the southern hemisphere) the right-hand flash is used in the morning when the sun is coming up from the east, and the left-hand one fills in the shadows as the sun moves towards the western horizon in the evening. Electronic flash is ideal. Even when using a flash fill-in attention should be paid to the background, for bright branches and leaves may be very distracting and should be removed.

The background problem becomes acute when working in the tree-tops since the glaring branches behind the nest form a definite distraction. Little can be done about this in many situations; it is impossible to clamber out to the offending limbs and no use waiting for dull days—they may take months to materialize. Some improvement may be possible by printing-in the denser portions of the negative during enlargement, by over-exposure and under-development, or by over-exposing and after-treating the negatives with a reducer of the ammonium persulphate type which reduces contrast without eliminating shadow detail.

### Combating Heat

Hides can get abominably hot even in the sun of a comparatively mild northern summer; in the heat of the tropics they can be unbearable. The photographer cannot change the weather and the local birds are accustomed to the heat, breeding, sleeping and feeding despite it. Those who wish to photograph them must learn to combat the heat, and one way to do this is to work in the early morning before the sun has climbed too high in the sky. At this time of the day the birds themselves are most active. By midday and throughout the afternoon many species rest up in whatever shade they can find; bird photographers do the same. With very tame birds it may be possible to sling a fly sheet between trees to shade the hide and the nest as well.

Bags made from flax are used in hot climates for holding water; the gradual seepage and evaporation cools the contents if there is a good circulation of air, such as when the bag is fastened to the front of a moving vehicle. The same principle is used in the design of the "cool safe" used by travellers to keep meat and fats in some sort of condition. These "coolers" consist essentially of a metal box

---

IN THE TROPICS. Films and plates may be washed in a river or tidal estuary by driving in stakes and making a frame on which to hang or loop them (1). In the dry season water is a great attraction to birds, as it is to other creatures, and a water hole makes a good site for "wait and see" pictures (2); or a dripping water bag or can may be hung in a bush or tree (4). A supply of cool drinking water for the photographer is ensured by hanging a flax water bag on the hide; evaporation lowers the temperature (3). A cool safe for materials may consist of a tin draped with a wet cloth (5); and in waterless desert regions a hole in the ground uncovered to the cold night air, and covered again before sunrise, remains cool during the heat of the following day (6).

covered with hessian on to which a trickle of water falls to keep the whole thing moist. Evaporation from all sides keeps the inside temperature well below that of the surroundings. On very hot days I have sometimes fixed a water-bag on the cross-wires at the back of the hide to provide cool drinks when they were needed.

In the hot season direct sunlight can quickly destroy eggs and chicks; these should be shaded while the camera is being set up or removed.

Heat saps one's energy and flies are perhaps just as exhausting. Fortunately, in dry areas at least, when it is really hot (shade temperatures of 105°F. and over) the flies are usually dead or dormant. Flies inside hides can be maddening; I spray the latter inside and out, and particularly round the peepholes, with a DDT insecticide before each session. Insect repellents containing dimethyl-phthalate smeared on to the skin are also good, though their effectiveness wears off quickly in hot weather. A fly net to droop from your hat over the face wards off many insects that would otherwise crawl into your ears, eyes and nostrils. These nets are a boon also when working in the open or tramping through the bush in search of nests.

### Care of Materials and Equipment

Heat and humidity can cause havoc with photographic gear and materials. Of the two humidity is the worst. Films and plates may be stored in sealed tins inside a cool safe of the kind already described. This is quite effective provided that there is an adequate supply of water (not necessarily fit for drinking purposes, and when humidity is not high enough to prevent evaporation), or in parts of the tropics, more especially inland continental regions where days are hot and nights surprisingly cold. This can be turned to advantage when storing film. A pit is dug in the ground and in this the sensitive material is kept. After dark the hole is uncovered to allow the night air to cool the contents. In the morning, before the sun has risen, the pit is re-covered with blankets, hides or some other suitable material so that the cool air is retained and the same procedure is followed each evening. If a

RED-EARED FIRETAIL. This exotic Australian bird, never before photographed, provides a good example of synchro-sunlight technique. The harsh sunlight of the tropics gives extreme contrast and it is necessary to throw light into the shadows, the flashgun being ideal for this. Here a single flash film was used at camera level and the lens aperture set so that the sunlight and the flash contributed about equal shares to the exposure.—*Photo:* John Warham.

BROWN HONEYEATER AND FLAME GREVILLEA (*above, left*). Twin flash tubes here gave a soft lighting, although there was brilliant sunlight, and made the subject stand out from the background.—*Photo:* John Warham.

SPLENDID BLUE WREN (*above, right*). Similar technique to that used for the brown honeyeater, but only one flash tube was used a little above camera level to throw the feather detail into slight relief.—*Photo:* John Warham.

LESSER NODDY TERNS (*opposite*). A rare bird photographed in mangroves in Australia. Swing back was used to bring the rear bird's head into the focal plane.— *Photo:* John Warham.

PARROT. This comical subject is emerging from its nest hole in a stump of a tree.—
*Photo:* John Warham.

LILY-TROTTER. The toes of this bird are four inches long and distribute its weight over a wide area to enable it to walk over soft water plants.—*Photo:* W. T. Miller.

DARTER, OR SNAKE BIRD (*above*). The type of picture to be secured by carrying a camera at the ready.—*Photo:* W. T. Miller.

HUMMING BIRD (*opposite*). The speedflash has effectively "stopped" the very rapid wing movement. The bird is interested in the flowers, not the bee; it takes the nectar whilst hovering.—*Photo:* Fletcher.

THREE OSTRICHES. In contrast to the humming bird (*p. 167*), which is the smallest member of the bird world, the ostrich is the largest. A picture taken in their homeland of South Africa.—*Photo:* R. T. Elliott.

vehicle can be parked over the hole during the day shading it from the direct rays of the sun, so much the better. Occasionally caves can be put to use, for these are often cool even on the hottest day.

It is necessary to be constantly on the alert to see that cameras and sensitive equipment like exposure meters are not left in the sun. Metal cameras become too hot to hold in a few minutes and such treatment will damage shutters, melt lens cements, and fog the film. Wooden dark slides also tend to buckle and gape under hot and humid conditions: single metal plate holders are more reliable. All photographic sensitive material used should be tropically packed—film generally in small metal containers—and the seals should not be broken until just before use.

*Colour in the Tropics*

To work in colour is a "must" for the wild life photographer in the tropics with so many brightly-hued birds to be taken. Lots of these are deliberate in their movements—for example parrots and macaws—and give plenty of opportunities of shots with little risk of losses due to restlessness. With strong lighting short exposures may be given but contrasty situations have to be guarded against. If these are encountered small flashbulbs are the answer, enabling the contrast range to be brought within bounds. Blue bulbs are needed with daylight-type film. This method has, of course, a general application, but in Europe the contrasts are far less extravagant owing to the greater luminosity of the shadows. A few trial exposures are required to establish the correct stop and shutter speed ratios; once more, to avoid over-flashing, the shutter speed should be sufficient to give a true rendering of the background and the stop correct for the flash.

Colour film needs processing fairly soon after exposure if fading of the image and faulty renderings are to be avoided. When working in the wilds processing is usually out of the question and often the temperature of available water supplies is too high, particularly with Agfacolor and Ferraniacolor which must be developed at 65°F. Sometimes the exposed film can be stored in the refrigerator of a nearby homestead or settlement; if not the cool safe may be used. I keep colour film in an airtight stainless steel developing tank and this can either be put in a refrigerator if such is available, in the cool safe, or even in a canvas bucket filled with water. Exposed material may be sent by air to the nearest city for refrigerated storage. Large photographic wholesalers usually have cool rooms and may be willing to store film until the photographer can get back to collect and process it.

Frequently the only answer is to send the exposed material direct by air to the nearest processing house, and this is really the only solution when very humid conditions combined with temperatures in the nineties prevail. When packing up exposed film for posting and storage it is important that it should be as free from moisture as possible, otherwise condensation may occur during cold storage and the pictures may be marred by blotches on the emulsion. For this reason films should be packed up for despatch only on dry days. In my experience exposed Ektachrome will keep unimpaired for two months if kept in a cool safe, but in humid conditions it is doubtful if this would be possible. Humidity can be countered to some extent by storing the films in an airtight metal box in which silica gel is kept. The "telltale" variety is best and when this has changed colour it is replaced by a fresh supply, and the other regenerated by heat.

### Processing in the Field

Nature photographers in the tropics are often away from "base" for months at a time. On several counts it is inadvisable to keep exposed black-and-white materials for long before developing them. There is the danger that the latent image may fade and fogging take place, and also that some defect in the equipment may pass unnoticed until too late—a faulty shutter, for example. If a selection at least of the exposures are processed on the spot then any necessary retakes can be made.

Assuming some sort of night-time darkroom can be rigged up, the chief difficulty arises when the available water supplies get above about 80°F., as very often happens. Development is done after dark, and if the temperature falls appreciably during the night, developers and other solutions are made up during the day and put outside so that they cool down in the night air. Several buckets of water for washing are also cooled, since it is important that all processing solutions and the water for the first few washes should be at about the same temperature or reticulation is probable.

Development is followed by a chrome-alum hardener bath, fixer and finally washing. If water is scarce it may be sufficient to give just a few washes, or a hypo-eliminator may be used. Films are then dried, rolled up in black photographic paper and put back in their metal containers. They are rewashed when more favourable conditions are encountered.

When the temperature of the developer cannot be reduced below 90–95°F. the films and plates must be prehardened, and this is followed by a M.Q. developer loaded with sodium sulphate according to the manufacturer's recommendations.

Films and plates can often be washed satisfactorily in streams, rivers, and even in sea-water. When washing in rivers and streams I usually construct a frame from branches within which the developed films are stretched horizontally between film clips. The frame can be covered with the fine gauge copper gauze used for fly-proofing windows; this prevents any large particles of leaves or debris touching the emulsion. Sea-water is effective but it is not often possible to put the films in the sea on account of the waves and the danger of sand abrasions; the water must be bucketed out (canvas ones are best) and the films washed by hand.

# A Guide to British Birds

THE FOLLOWING TABLES are intended to provide a guide to the beginner in bird photography. In particular the camera distances are suggested ones and it is not intended that they should be strictly adhered to, although they are based on experience and will be found useful in estimating the possibilities of photography at any particular nest site.

### Working Days

Here are listed the approximate number of days which elapse between the time the hide may be erected and the time the young leave the nest—that is, the approximate number of working days available for photography. With chicks that stay in the nest for a while and then wander off—as happens with nightjars and some gulls—this has been allowed for. Where the young leave the nest as soon as they are dry, for example ducks and waders, it is assumed that hide making will not be attempted until the eggs are half incubated. Thus the figures in this column represent half of the normal incubation periods for the particular species concerned.

### $6\frac{1}{2}$ in. Lens

This is assumed to be used with a $2\frac{1}{4}$ in. square or $2\frac{1}{2} \times 3\frac{1}{2}$ in. film or plate, and the distances ensure a $1\frac{1}{4}$-in. long image of the bird photographed sideways on to the camera.

### 8 in. Lens

The negative size is here assumed to be quarter-plate, and the length of the image of the bird about $1\frac{1}{2}$ in.

## 9 cm. and 13.5 cm. Lenses

These are probably the most useful focal lengths for the 24 × 36 mm. negative of the 35 mm. miniature camera. The distances in both cases will provide an image of the bird 15–16 mm. long.

## Maximum Exposure

The exposure times given are the longest that may be tried with the bird standing at its nest. If it is sitting much longer ones may be practicable.

## The Birds

The birds are divided into groups, which it is thought may best assist the photographer—the first group a selection for the beginner, and the remaining groups arranged according to habitat. The complete selection of birds covered is as follows:—

| Species | Work Days | Camera Distance (ft.) | | | | Max. Exp. (sec.) |
| --- | --- | --- | --- | --- | --- | --- |
| | | 2¼ sq. — ¼ pl. 6½ in. | 8 in. | 35 mm. 9 cm. | 13.5 cm. | |
| CHAFFINCH. Neat mossy cup with pale reddish marked eggs in hedges and bushes 4–7 ft. up. Careful "gardening" often needed. | 14 | 3½ | 4 | 3½ | 6 | 1/5 |
| COMMON WHITETHROAT. Basket nest with grey-brown eggs in vegetation by streams, in bracken, in bushes and hedges. Tame. Careful trimming needed as nest flimsy. Perches readily. | 12 | 3½ | 4 | 3½ | 6 | 1/5 |
| GREAT TIT. White, red-spotted eggs in holes in trees and elsewhere, beneath roofs and in nest boxes. Tame. Rapid movements. Perches readily. | 19 | 3½ | 4 | 3½ | 6 | 1/25 |
| GREENFINCH. Greenish spotted eggs in cup nest in hedges and bushes 5–10 ft. up. Not difficult. Fairly long waits between feeds when young big. | 14 | 3½ | 4 | 3½ | 6 | 1/5 |
| LAPWING. Four pointed olive-brown mottled eggs on sparse lining of straws on ground in meadows or arable land. Must be worked on eggs. Choose nest overlooked by farm etc. for safety. | 14 | 6½ | 7 | 6 | 10 | 1 |
| ROBIN. Buff mottled eggs in nest on ground, in holes in banks, walls etc. Confiding, stands motionless and perches readily. | 14 | 3½ | 4 | 3½ | 6 | 1 |
| SONG THRUSH. Blue, black-spotted eggs in mud-lined nest in hedges and bushes 4–7 ft. up. May be wary but stands still. | 14 | 5 | 5½ | 5 | 9 | 1/2 |

CHAFFINCH. Male has handsome slate-blue head, chestnut back, prominent white shoulder patch, white wing bar and white on the outer tail feathers. Tail and wings blackish. Female duller; light brown above, dull white below. Our most numerous bird. Length 6 in.

COMMON WHITETHROAT. Both sexes have a noticeable reddish-brown tinge to the wing and a white throat. Male wears a grey cap, female a brown one; outer tail feathers are white. Feathers of the crown are often raised to form a slight crest when the bird is excited. A summer visitor. Length 5½ in.

GREAT TIT. The biggest of the common titmice. Crown and throat are glossy black, and a black band joins the two areas enclosing a white cheek-patch. Breast yellow with a broad black band running from throat to belly. Back yellowish green, wings and tail blue-grey. Wings are crossed by a thin white bar; outer tail feathers white. Female slightly duller than male. Length 5½ in.

GREENFINCH. Male has dark olive-green plumage with bright yellow on the rump and yellow patches on the wing quills and sides of the tail. Female is similar to male but considerably duller and the yellow less pronounced. Both have typical conical beaks of the finch tribe. Length 6 in.

ROBIN. Olive-brown on the back with bright orange breast, throat and forehead, this most familiar of birds needs no further description. Both sexes are alike. Young birds lack the orange breast and have spotted underparts, but have typical robin-like stance and mannerisms. Length 5½ in.

LAPWING. In the air the broad rounded wings and slow wing beats combined with black and white colouring are distinguishing features. At close quarters, the long crest, white belly, black breast and dark greenish back and flanks showing metallic green and purplish reflections. There is an area of orange-buff below the tail. Sexes similar. Length 12 in.

| Species | Work Days | Camera Distance (ft.) | | | | Max. Exp. |
| | | 2¼ sq. — ¼ pl. 6½ in. | 8 in. | 35 mm. 9 cm. | 13.5 cm. | (sec.) |
|---|---|---|---|---|---|---|
| STARLING. Blue eggs in nest beneath eaves, in holes in buildings, trees etc. Small pylon hide may be needed. Restless—skill needed to stop movement. | 20 | 5 | 5½ | 5 | 9 | 1/10 |
| SWALLOW. White, red-spotted eggs in mud nest supported on beams in outbuildings. Confiding but restless. Flash generally needed. Second brood often reared in same nest. | 14 | 4 | 4½ | 4 | 7 | 1/25 |

SONG THRUSH. Warm brown on back, head and wings; upper breast and flanks flushed with a rich buff, belly shading to a light cream. Breast marked with brown spots shaped like arrowheads. Carriage usually upright. Sexes are similar. Length 9 in.

BLUE TIT. Bright blue crown, white cheeks and sulphur belly easily identify this common bird. There is blue on the wings and tail and the back is yellow-green. Sexes are similar but females generally duller. Length 4½ in.

STARLING. Clothed in glossy black feathers which bear metallic blue, green and red reflections. Feathers are tipped buffish to give both breast and back a spotted appearance. Tail is short and bill rather long and pointed, and in flight the bird has a characteristic arrow-like outline. Sexes alike. Length 8½ in.

BLACKCAP. A small greyish brown bird, male having prominent glossy black cap coming down to eye, and female a ginger one. Underparts grey in male and brownish-grey in female. Beak rather slender. Song is a rich warble and the alarm a hard scolding, like two small stones knocked together. Length 5½ in.

BLACKBIRD. Male has glossy black plumage and yellow bill; female dull brown on the back and warmer brown below mottled with darker brown. Carries itself less upright than song thrush, and when alighting raises tail momentarily. Utters noisy rattling cries when alarmed. Length 10 in.

SWALLOW. Long forked tail, slender outline and long wings suffice to identify it on the wing. General colour of upper parts is glossy blue-black, chestnut throat and forehead, and light buffish underparts. Females usually have somewhat shorter streamers to their tails. Length 7 in.

| Species | Work Days | Camera Distance (ft.) | | | | Max. Exp. |
| | | 2¼ sq. — ¼ pl. 6½ in. | 8 in. | 35 mm. 9 cm. | 13.5 cm. | (sec.) |
|---|---|---|---|---|---|---|
| BLACKBIRD. Greenish, brown-mottled eggs in firm cup nest in bush, hedge or fork 4–7 ft. up. Often timid; deliberate in movements. Full exposure for feather detail. | 14 | 5½ | 6 | 5½ | 9 | 1/2 |
| BLACKCAP. Buff, brown-blotched eggs in basket nest of bents fixed in bush or bramble 3–5 ft. up. Usually fairly tame. Care with trimming as nest often poorly supported. | 12 | 3½ | 4 | 3½ | 6 | 1/5 |
| BLUE TIT. White, red-spotted eggs in nest in hole in tree or wall. Tame but very restless. Perches. | 16 | 3½ | 3½ | 3½ | 5 | 1/25 |
| BULLFINCH. Blue, spotted eggs in fine nest of roots in bush or bramble 4–7 ft. up. Often tame. | 14 | 3½ | 4 | 3½ | 6 | 1/5 |
| GARDEN WARBLER. Buff, grey-blotched eggs in basket nest in bush, bracken etc. 3–5 ft. up. Usually fairly tame. Care with trimming as nest often poorly supported. | 10 | 3½ | 4 | 3½ | 6 | 1/5 |
| HEDGE SPARROW. Bright blue egg in cup nest low down in hedge, bush or bramble. Difficult to show well on account of jerky movements. | 13 | 3½ | 4 | 3½ | 6 | 1/25 |
| LINNET. White, red-spotted eggs in cup nest fixed in bush or hedge 4–6 ft. up. | 12 | 3½ | 4 | 3½ | 6 | 1/10 |
| LONG-TAILED TIT. White, red-spotted eggs in domed moss and lichen nest hung in honeysuckle or bushes 2–6 ft. up. Very tame but rapid in movement. Perches readily. | 15 | 3½ | 4 | 3½ | 6 | 1/25 |

**BULLFINCH.** A plump and rather retiring bird. Male is quite unmistakable on account of its rose-red underparts. Head capped with glossy black, back grey, and wings and tail black. There is a white patch above the tail. Bill heavy and conical. Female is similar, but breast is greyish-pink, not red as in the male. Length 6 in.

**MISTLE THRUSH.** The biggest of our resident thrushes. Much greyer than the song thrush and easily distinguished from it by white tips to the outer tail feathers; also spots on breast are bigger and broader, and flight is undulating owing to the regular closure of the wings. Sexes similar. Length 10½ in.

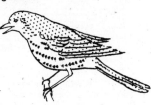

**LINNET.** A small finch with cleft tail and conical bill. Male has a warm chestnut back, greyish head and crimson crown and breast. Female is much duller and has streaked underparts. Distinguished from similar redpoll by lack of a black patch on the chin. Length 5 in.

**HEDGE SPARROW.** A dull, plump and decidedly inconspicuous little bird. Breast, head and throat are grey, remainder of feathers warm brown. Bill is slender, not conical as in house sparrow, to which it is not related. Sexes similar. Length 6 in.

**NIGHTINGALE.** A skulking robin-like species with even russet-brown head and back and greyish-brown underparts. Tail even more rufous than the back. Throat and belly whitish. Has a croaking alarm, and male's song is heard both by day and night. Sexes are similar in plumage. Length 6½ in.

**GARDEN WARBLER.** This rather pale bird has no outstanding features. It is rather plump and has a somewhat stouter beak than the other warblers. Upper parts brownish, underparts pale buff. Eye rather large and dark. Sexes alike. Song an even and rather restrained warble. Length 5½ in.

**LONG-TAILED TIT.** A small bird with very long tail. Plumage pattern somewhat haphazard; pinks, dirty white and blacks predominate. Wings and tail blackish and the white in the outermost tail feathers is very obvious. An active and confiding species often seen in parties and in company with other kinds of titmice. Sexes alike. Length 5½ in. of which 3 in. is tail.

| Species | Work Days | Camera Distance (ft.) | | | | Max. Exp. (sec.) |
|---|---|---|---|---|---|---|
| | | 2¼ sq. — ¼ pl. 6½ in. | 8 in. | 35 mm. 9 cm. | 13.5 cm. | |
| MISTLE THRUSH. Buff mottled eggs in firm cup nest in fork of tree 6–15 ft. up. Pylon hide usually required. | 14 | 5½ | 6 | 5½ | 9 | 1/2 |
| NIGHTINGALE. Olive eggs in nest of leaves close to ground in thorn bush or bramble. Stands quite still. Prefers dense cover where light poor. | 12 | 4 | 4½ | 4 | 6 | 1/2 |
| TURTLE DOVE. White eggs on flimsy twig platform in bush about 5–12 ft. up. Very timid, no hide till eggs hatched. Often deserts if disturbed from eggs. | 18 | 6½ | 7 | 6½ | 10 | 1 |
| WILLOW WARBLER. White, red-spotted eggs in domed nest on ground beneath clump of grass. Tame. | 14 | 3½ | 4 | 3½ | 6 | 1/10 |
| WREN. White, red-spotted eggs in domed nest fixed in dry bracken, ivy, holes in walls, etc. Tame. | 16 | 3½ | 3½ | 3½ | 5 | 1/10 |
| YELLOW-HAMMER. Pale, brown-scribbled eggs in nest of bents in bush, hedge or on ground or bank. | 12 | 4 | 4½ | 4 | 6 | 1/5 |

**TURTLE DOVE.** Head and neck ashy grey, back brown, wings rufous brown with black centres to the feathers, and underparts and throat pale vinous. There is a prominent group of black and white bands running across the sides of the neck. Tail black, and the broad white tips are very obvious in flight. Sexes similar. Length 11 in.

**WREN.** A very small, russet-brown bird whose short tail is usually cocked up at an acute angle. Sides, wings and tail are noticeably barred. An excitable and very active bird with a whirring, almost insect-like flight, and remarkably loud vehement song made up of a series of trills. Sexes similar. Length 3¾ in.

**WILLOW WARBLER.** A small, slim bird, olive-green above, yellow-green below. There is a light stripe above eye. Distinguished from very similar chiffchaff by light brown legs instead of black and by soft liquid song of male, whereas chiffchaff calls its name repeatedly. Bill fine and slender. Sexes similar. Length 4 in.

**DABCHICK.** A tiny, almost tailless water bird whose body is not much bigger than a clenched fist. Plumage of upper parts is dark brown with chestnut on the cheeks and throat. There is a bright yellow green mark on base of the bill, which is short, stout and straight. The bird dives readily when feeding or if frightened. They are seldom seen in flight. Sexes similar. Length 10½ in.

**YELLOW-HAMMER.** Head, face and underparts of male are bright yellow, upper parts chestnut streaked with black, rump chestnut. Outer tail feathers white. Female much duller with little yellow on head but a good deal on belly. "Little bit of bread and no cheese" song easily recognized. Length 6½ in.

**KINGFISHER.** Brilliant blue upper parts, warm chestnut breast and bright red legs make this brightest of our birds quite unmistakable. Has a short tail and long but stout beak, and direct darting flight. Blue plumage changes to green when viewed from certain angles. Sexes alike. Length 6½ in.

| Species | Work Days | 2¼ sq. — ¼ pl. | | 35 mm. | | Max. Exp. |
| --- | --- | --- | --- | --- | --- | --- |
| | | 6½ in. | 8 in. | 9 cm. | 13.5 cm. | (sec.) |
| COOT. Buff, black-spotted eggs in shallow nest of rushes etc. at water level. Common but reluctant to face occupied hide. Best results when eggs starting to chip. | 12 | 7½ | 8½ | 7½ | 12 | 1/5 |
| DABCHICK. Yellowish, stained eggs on floating nest of damp weeds at edge of lake; not in running water. Must be worked on eggs. | 10 | 6½ | 7 | 6½ | 10 | 1/5 |
| KINGFISHER. White eggs in chamber bored in river bank. Takes readily to properly placed perch. | 25 | 3½ | 4 | 3½ | 6 | 1/2 |
| MALLARD. Large white eggs in loose nest of down and grass on ground beneath brush or coarse vegetation. Often well away from water. Timid, must be worked on eggs. | 15 | 7½ | 9 | 7½ | 13 | 1/10 |
| PIED WAGTAIL. Grey, speckled eggs in loose cup nest under cover in woodpiles, outbuildings, ledges and holes. Moving tail chief problem. | 14 | 4 | 4½ | 4 | 6 | 1/25 |
| REDSHANK. Buff, brown-marked eggs in shallow nest of sedge etc. on ground in damp meadows and bogs. Must be worked on eggs. | 12 | 5 | 5½ | 5 | 8 | 1/10 |
| REED BUNTING. Pale brown, black-scrawled eggs in cup nest in coarse grass and low bushes 1–14 ft. up. Usually tame. Nest sites very contrasty. | 12 | 3½ | 4 | 3½ | 6 | 1/5 |
| SEDGE WARBLER. Freckled buff eggs in rough cup nest low down in waterside weeds. Tame. | 14 | 3½ | 4 | 3½ | 6 | 1/5 |

COOT. A heavy, stumpy water bird. Plumage grey-black relieved only by a striking white bill and frontal shield. Legs greenish. Length 15 in.

REDSHANK. A wading bird with long orange-red legs, warm brown back and head streaked with black. In flight, white rump and white crescent on trailing edge of wing show up clearly. This bird is easily alarmed and bobs up and down before flying off with a piping "tew, tew, tew" note. Length 11 in.

SEDGE WARBLER. A small brownish bird with black streaks on crown and back. Underparts cream coloured, flanks buffish. Prominent creamy eye-stripe and streaked crown serve to distinguish this bird from less common reed warbler. Sexes similar. An active bird which clings easily to stems of reeds, osiers and similar plants. Length 5 in.

REED BUNTING. Both sexes have brown backs streaked darker brown, small conical bills and fairly long tails with white outermost feathers. Male has a black head and throat and a white collar round back of neck. Female has brown head, a buffish stripe from below and behind the eye and a blackish moustache-like streak below the bill. Underparts whitish in male, pale buff in female, more or less streaked with brown on the flanks. Length 6 in.

PIED WAGTAIL. Our only small black and white bird with a long tail which is continually moved up and down. Male has crown and back, throat and upper breast black, forehead, cheeks and belly white. Wings are crossed by two white bars and outer tail feathers are white. Female is similar but tends to be grey and white rather than black and white. Length 7 in.

MALLARD. The drake has a dark green head and white collar round neck. The back and belly are a pale grey and breast purplish-brown. The central feathers of the otherwise whitish tail are black and curled upwards. Female is quite different, a brownish speckled bird with a lighter eyestripe. Both sexes have a characteristic violet speculum bordered by a stripe of white, and then one of black on both sides. Length 23 in.

| Species | Work Days | Camera Distance (ft.) | | | | Max. Exp. (sec.) |
|---|---|---|---|---|---|---|
| | | 2¼ sq. — ¼ pl. 6½ in. | 8 in. | 35 mm. 9 cm. | 13.5 cm. | |
| SNIPE. Light brown eggs, mottled with darker-brown, in shallow nest of sedge etc. on ground in damp meadows and bogs. Must be worked on eggs. | 10 | 5 | 5½ | 5½ | 8 | 1/10 |
| SKYLARK. Speckled drab-grey eggs in cup nest hidden in grass on meadow land. | 10 | 4 | 4½ | 4 | 6 | 1/5 |
| TUFTED DUCK. Large white eggs in nest of dark down and grass etc. on ground in water-side cover. Timid. Must be worked on eggs. | 12 | 7½ | 8½ | 7½ | 12 | 1/10 |
| WATERHEN. Buff, black - spotted eggs in loose cup of sedge under cover of water-side vegetation, usually a little above water level. Common, but very reluctant to face occupied hide. Best results when eggs starting to chip. | 11 | 6½ | 7½ | 6½ | 11 | 1/10 |
| YELLOW WAGTAIL. Olive eggs in small cup nest on ground beneath grass clump. Moving tail chief problem. | 13 | 4 | 4½ | 4 | 6 | 1/10 |

**WATERHEN.** Also known as Moorhen. A perky and restless water-bird with brownish-black plumage and a bright red frontal shield. There is a series of slanting white stripes on the flanks, and the constantly cocked tail is edged with white. Legs green. Sexes similar. Length 13 in.

**SNIPE.** Has very long straight bill and richly marked upper parts barred with black, brown and buff so that bird appears to be striped the length of the back. Crown is black, streaked with black and tawny-brown; long legs greenish. Sexes are similar; length 10½ in. of which 2½ in. is the bill.

**SKYLARK.** A brownish bird with a fairly prominent eye-stripe and distinct crest on head. Tail long and outer tail feathers are white. Feathers of back edged with whitish and giving bird a rather streaky appearance; underparts whitish or buffish, flanks and throat streaked with brown. Noted for male's soaring song flight. Sexes similar. Length 7 in.

**TUFTED DUCK.** A squat, short-tailed duck. In the male the whole of the body is black except for the flanks and underparts, which are pure white. In the female the upper parts are dark brown and the flanks and underparts less white. Both have a loose tuft of feathers hanging down from back of head. Eye is bright yellow. A broad white wing bar is also visible in flight. Length 17 in.

**YELLOW WAGTAIL.** Very slim, long tailed bird seldom seen perched other than on the ground. Breast is a bright yellow, back greenish. Male has very bright yellow head. Wings and tail blackish brown; outermost tail feathers white. Female is duller, the yellow is paler and the back browner. Both sexes distinguished from grey wagtail by much shorter tails and lack of grey on back and head. Length 6½ in.

**BLACK-HEADED GULL.** A medium sized gull which wears a dark-brown hood in the breeding season. Bill and legs red. This is the commonest gull to be seen inland, where it often follows the plough or chases flying insects. Sexes similar. Length 14½ in.

| Species | Work Days | Camera Distance (ft.) | | | | Max. Exp. (sec.) |
|---|---|---|---|---|---|---|
| | | 2¼ sq. — ¼ pl. 6½ in. | 8 in. | 35 mm. 9 cm. | 13.5 cm. | |
| BLACK - HEADED GULL. Greenish - brown, dark - blotched eggs in shallow nest on sandhills, seashore bogs, sewage farms. Frequents boggy ground. Colonies often very large. | 18 | 6½ | 7 | 6½ | 10 | 1 |
| CURLEW. Large, olive brown - blotched eggs on ground in heather or rough pasture. Usually rather timid; must be worked at eggs. | 15 | 8½ | 10 | 8½ | 15 | 1 |
| DIPPER. White eggs in large mossy domed nest under banks and waterfalls. Always near mountain stream. Usually tame. | 20 | 4 | 4½ | 4 | 6 | 1/25 |
| GREY WAGTAIL. Pale eggs in cup nest under stone by fast flowing rocky streams. Usually tame; wagging tail a problem. | 12 | 4 | 4½ | 4 | 6 | 1/25 |
| MEADOW PIPPIT. Greyish eggs in cup nest on ground beneath grass clump etc. | 14 | 3½ | 4 | 3½ | 6 | 1/10 |
| MERLIN. Round, red-speckled eggs on ground beneath heather. Nests neither abundant nor easily discovered. Low hide best. | 21 | 6½ | 7 | 6½ | 10 | 1/5 |
| RED GROUSE. Buff, black-marked eggs on ground amongst heather or bracken. Low hide, well concealed. Worked at eggs. | 11 | 6½ | 7 | 6½ | 10 | 1 |
| RING OUZEL. Greenish, brown-marked eggs in cup of grasses on ground beneath bracken, heather or stones. Full exposure needed for feather detail. | 14 | 5½ | 6 | 5½ | 9 | 1/2 |
| WHEATEAR. Blue eggs in hole in ground or stone wall. Wagging tail chief problem. | 15 | 3½ | 4 | 3½ | 6 | 1/10 |

**CURLEW.** A large wader with streaky brown plumage and very long down-curved beak. Rump white, tail barred dark brown, long legs greenish-grey. Liquid flute-like voice quite distinct. Sexes similar. Length 22–23 in., of which 5 in. is beak.

**MERLIN.** The smallest of our hawks. Upper parts are grey-blue, the nape is warm buff and the under parts brownish-buff streaked darker. Tail has a broad black band. Does not hover but has dashing flight close to the ground. Female considerably larger than male. Length: male 10½ in.; female 12½ in.

**GREY WAGTAIL.** The only water-haunting bird having yellow underparts and very long tail. Back and head are slate-grey; male has a black throat in breeding season, female a whitish one. Length 7 in.

**DIPPER.** A short-tailed plump bird which looks like a large wren. Upper parts are dark brown. The white front merges into a chestnut band and this again into the black of the belly. Perches frequently on stones in mid-stream where it bobs up and down in a characteristic fashion. Sexes alike. Length 7 in.

**MEADOW PIPIT.** A small lark-like bird, brown above with darker markings; lighter below with streaked breast and white outer tail feathers. No crest on head as with the skylark. Mainly seen on the ground. Sexes similar. Length 6 in.

**RED GROUSE.** A rather large, plump, dark red-brown bird. There is a bright red wattle above the eye and the feathered legs are white. Plumage varies considerably according to the season and locality. Flight is strong, close to the ground and the grouse glides with wings curved downwards. Length 13–15 in.

187

| Species | Work Days | Camera Distance (ft.) | | | | Max. Exp. (sec.) |
|---|---|---|---|---|---|---|
| | | $2\frac{1}{4}$ sq. — $\frac{1}{4}$ pl. | | 35 mm. | | |
| | | $6\frac{1}{2}$ in. | 8 in. | 9 cm. | 13.5 cm. | |
| CARRION CROW. Greenish, grey-marked eggs in large nest. Solitary. A wary bird. | 30 | 8 | 10 | 8 | 15 | 1/2 |
| GREATER SPOTTED WOODPECKER. White eggs in cavity bored in tree trunk. Entrance 7 ft. and more in height. Clings motionless to trunk. Allow for thickness of bird when focusing. | 20 | $5\frac{1}{2}$ | 6 | $5\frac{1}{2}$ | 9 | 1 |
| GREEN WOODPECKER. White eggs in cavity bored in tree trunk. Entrance 7 ft. and more in height. Clings motionless to trunk. Allow for thickness of bird when focusing. | 20 | $6\frac{1}{2}$ | 7 | $6\frac{1}{2}$ | 10 | 1 |
| KESTREL. Round, brick-red eggs in hollow tree, hole in ruin, old crows nest etc. Pylon needed. May be worked on hard-set eggs. | 34 | $7\frac{1}{2}$ | 9 | $7\frac{1}{2}$ | 13 | 1/2 |
| ROOK. Olive, brown - blotched eggs in huge stick nest in tops of trees. Colonial. Difficulty in finding position overlooking nest. Hide framework may be built in winter as nests used each year. | 30 | 8 | 10 | 8 | 15 | 1/2 |
| SPARROW - HAWK. Pale red-blotched eggs in self-built nest in trees from 15 ft. upwards. Pylon needed. May be worked on hard-set eggs. | 31 | $7\frac{1}{2}$ | $7\frac{1}{2}$ | 9 | 13 | 1/2 |
| TREE CREEPER. Red-spotted white eggs in shallow nest fitted behind loose bark against tree trunk. Tame but very active. | 14 | $3\frac{1}{2}$ | 4 | $3\frac{1}{2}$ | 6 | 1/25 |
| WOODPIGEON. White eggs on shallow twig platform in bushes and trees from 6 ft. up. Choose a low nest. Must not be flushed till eggs hatched or desertion probable. About 4 hours between feeds. Very wary. | 28 | $7\frac{1}{2}$ | 9 | $7\frac{1}{2}$ | 13 | 1 |

**WHEATEAR.** Male is grey above, with blackish wings and white underparts. There is a black mark below and behind the eye, broadly edged with white above. Female is browner above and much buffer below, the wings dark brown. She has a light eye stripe but no black mark. Rump and base of tail in both sexes are white, and this enables the birds to be distinguished at a glance even from a distance. There is a broad black band across the end of the tail. Length 6 in.

**RING OUZEL.** This bird has the stance and general appearance of a blackbird, but has an unmistakable white crescent on the breast. In the male the colours are cleaner and bolder than in the female; latter has narrower and slightly brownish crescent. Length 9½ in.

**CARRION CROW.** Uniformly black in plumage, with black bill and rather sleek appearance which distinguish it from otherwise similar rook. Carrion crows are usually solitary, rooks gregarious. Sexes similar. Length 18½ in.

**GREEN WOODPECKER.** The largest and noisiest of the woodpeckers, having a loud laughing cry. Predominant colour is green—dark above, lighter below, and it has a crimson crown. The male also has a black-edged crimson moustachial stripe; in the female this is black. Tail short and spiky, flight undulating. Length 12½ in.

**GREATER SPOTTED WOODPECKER.** Smaller than the green woodpecker and quite different in plumage pattern. Present bird has strongly pied appearance and black crown. There is a crimson patch on the nape in male birds and this is missing in the females. The wings are boldly barred with black and white. Length 9 in.

**KESTREL.** A small, reddish brown hawk, with characteristic hovering flight head into the wind as it scans the ground below for mice and insects. Male has blue-grey head and tail and chestnut upper parts spotted with black. Below it is buff streaked with dark brown. Female is less bright, and has a barred tail. Male's tail is crossed by a black band. Length 13½ in.

| Species | Work Days | Camera Distance (ft.) | | | | Max. Exp. (sec.) |
| --- | --- | --- | --- | --- | --- | --- |
| | | 2¼ sq. — ¼ pl. 6½ in. | 8 in. | 35 mm. 9 cm. | 13.5 cm. | |
| BUZZARD. Large, rounded, reddish-marked eggs in large nest on cliffs, or inland on crags and trees. Stands still except when feeding young. | 40 | 9 | 11 | 9 | 15 | 1 |
| COMMON TERN. Buffish, black-blotched egs on ground on beaches or islets. Colonial. Must be worked on eggs. | 16 | 6½ | 7 | 6½ | 10 | 1 |
| CORMORANT. Large whitish eggs in large flat twig and seaweed nest on rocks overlooking sea. Can often be stalked when near nest. Full exposure needed. | 30 | 12 | 14 | 12 | 20 | 1 |
| GREAT BLACK - BACKED GULL. Large brown, darkspotted eggs in shallow nest on ground on cliffs. Seldom many together. Hide required. | 35 | 9 | 10½ | 9 | 15 | 1 |
| GUILLEMOT. Blue, buff, green or other coloured egg, marked black, grey etc. and laid on narrow ledges overlooking sea. Many birds side by side. Allows close approach when with young. Nest often inaccessible to camera. Bird's constant movement of head makes exposure difficult. | 14 | 7 | 8 | 7 | 12 | 1 |
| HERRING GULL. Brown, chocolate-marked eggs in flat nest of weeds on rocks adjoining the sea. Hide needed but birds usually easy. | 32 | 8½ | 10 | 8½ | 15 | 1 |
| KITTIWAKE. Buff, grey and brown-marked eggs in seaweed nest on cliff ledges. Many together. Tame. Often difficult to find good viewpoint. | 30 | 7 | 8 | 7 | 12 | 1 |

**WOODPIGEON.** Biggest and commonest of our pigeons. Heavily built with blue-grey head, grey wings and back. The rump is blue grey and the tail dark grey. There is a white band across the wings and a white patch on either side of the neck, which also shows glossy green and purple reflections. Breast is vinous, belly pale grey. Sexes similar. Length 16 in.

**ROOK.** All black except for characteristic bare greyish white face and grey bill. Loose feathers on thighs create a baggy appearance to legs and serve to distinguish it from the carrion crow when on the ground. Sexes alike. Length 18 in.

**SPARROW-HAWK.** Dashing flight, long tail and broad rounded wings (not pointed as in the kestrel) serve to identify this hawk when seen in the air. Upper parts are dark grey, under parts strongly barred with dark-brown. Female is much larger, is brown rather than grey above but is less rufous below. Length: female 15 in., male 11½ in.

**BUZZARD.** A robust dark brown hawk whose lighter underparts are streaked with brown and white. The yellow legs are unfeathered. There is much variation in the plumage colours, but in flight the broad and rather rounded wings and broad rounded tail are distinctive as the bird soars in the sky. Sexes similar, but female usually the bigger of the two. Length 21 in.

**TREE CREEPER.** This is an inconspicuous mouse-like bird which is seen working up the trunks of trees searching for insects. Back, head and wings are brown and streaked with light buff; tail is brown and there is a light stripe above the eye. Under parts are whitish. Bill is thin, rather long and down-curved. Sexes similar. Length 5 in.

**CORMORANT.** A long-necked and large sea bird with bronze-brown back, and glossy black head and underparts. The birds have white chins and sides to the face. Eyes emerald green. In the breeding season cormorants also develop white patches on sides of thighs. Has a rather upright stance when settled on a rock or other perching place. Sexes similar. Length 36 in.

| Species | Work Days | Camera Distance (ft.) | | | | Max. Exp. |
| | | 2¼ sq. — ¼ pl. 6½ in. | 8 in. | 35 mm. 9 cm. | 13.5 cm. | (sec.) |
| --- | --- | --- | --- | --- | --- | --- |
| **OYSTER-CATCHER.** Brown, black - blotched eggs on ground amidst pebbles or vegetation. Often rather timid; worked at eggs. | 15 | 7 | 8 | 7 | 12 | 1/2 |
| **PUFFIN.** White egg down burrow below ground. Colonial. Prefers turfy sidings above the sea. Will usually allow a close approach without hide. | 40 | 6 | 6½ | 6 | 9 | 1 |
| **RAZORBILL.** Buff, black-marked egg on ground among rocky debris on cliffs. Nests in colonies. Will usually allow a close approach without hide. | 14 | 7 | 8 | 7 | 12 | 1 |
| **RINGED PLOVER.** Buff, black-spotted eggs laid on ground, lined with tiny stones, on sandy or pebbly beaches. Must be worked on eggs. Generally quite tame. | 12 | 4 | 5 | 4 | 7 | 1/2 |

PUFFIN. A squat sea bird with black head and back, white underparts. The legs and webbed feet are bright orange. Huge triangular bill, orange and yellow in colour. Spends much time on the surface of the sea. Sexes similar. Length 12 in.

OYSTER-CATCHER. A large bird with pied plumage, long orange bill and pinkish legs. Back, head and breast glossy black; underparts and a broad band across wing, white. A bird of noisy and excitable temperament using a variety of loud piping cries. Sexes similar. Length 17 in.

KITTIWAKE. The most lightly built of the gulls, white below and grey on back and wings. Legs black, bill rather slender and yellow in colour. Eye dark. Ends of wings are black. Tail white and rather square. Length 16 in.

HERRING GULL. The commonest gull round the coast of Britain; smaller than the great black back and with grey wings and back. Bill yellow with red spot on lower mandible. Legs flesh-coloured. Sexes similar. Length 22 in.

GUILLEMOT. Upper parts brown, underparts white. Black bill strong but pointed, a feature which, together with the more slender neck, easily serves to distinguish the species from the razorbill. The legs are brownish. Some birds have a white "spectacle" around the eye. Sexes similar. Length 16½ in.

COMMON TERN. Slender body, forked tail, thin pointed bill and pointed wings. Grey back and wings, white cheeks, breast and underparts, and a black cap. The long pointed bill is scarlet with a black tip. The short legs and feet are red. Sexes alike. Length 13½ in.

GREAT BLACK-BACKED GULL. The biggest of our gulls, with pure white head, neck, tail and underparts, and black wings. Legs are pale flesh-coloured or whitish. Back is black. Hatchet-shaped bill is yellow with a red patch on lower mandible. Sexes similar. Length 26 in.

| Species | Work Days | Camera Distance (ft.) | | | | Max. Exp. (sec.) |
|---|---|---|---|---|---|---|
| | | 2¼ sq. — ¼ pl. 6½ in. | 8 in. | 35 mm. 9 cm. | 13.5 cm. | |
| BARN OWL. White eggs laid in hollow trees, lofts in barns and church towers. | 60 | 7 | 8½ | 7 | 12 | 1 |
| LITTLE OWL. White eggs laid in hole in tree or masonry. Usually tame; stands still for several seconds. Perches readily. | 25 | 5 | 6 | 5 | 9 | 1 |
| LONG-EARED OWL. Eggs laid in old nest of crow, magpie or hawk. Least common of woodland owls. Prefers conifers. | 22 | 7½ | 9 | 7½ | 13 | 1 |
| NIGHTJAR. Rounded, white, brown - mottled eggs on ground: no nest. Prefers bracken covered patches in woods and commons. Site difficult to find. May be photographed by day when incubating. | 14 | 6 | 6½ | 6 | 9 | 1 |
| TAWNY OWL. White eggs laid in hole in tree or building, or in nest of crow or hawk. | 30 | 8 | 9 | 8 | 13 | 1 |

**RAZORBILL.** Has the black and white plumage of a typical auk. The black bill is deep and compressed and is crossed by a white line. Legs are black. Sexes alike. Length 16 in.

**RINGED PLOVER.** A small round-headed plover wearing a wide and prominent black collar round the white breast and neck. The head is boldly marked with white and black. Legs are yellowish, and in flight a narrow white wing bar is seen. Length 7½ in.

**LONG-EARED OWL.** A mottled greyish owl easily distinguished from other kinds if the ear tufts are erected. Noticeable yellow iris, and much greyer and more slender than the tawny owl. Sexes similar. Length 13½ in.

**BARN OWL.** The palest of our owls. Face and underparts pure white, back, head and wings a rich buff mottled and spotted with grey and white. Breast may carry a few small black spots. Sexes similar. Long legs. Length 13½ in.

**LITTLE OWL.** The smallest of our owls and is more often seen about in daytime than other species. Greyish-brown plumage spotted and barred with white. Sexes alike. Length 9 in.

**TAWNY OWL.** A large mottled bird usually of a warm-brown colour. Large black eyes and very well developed facial disc. Wings and tail strongly barred with dark brown. Has no ear tufts. This is the familiar hooting owl of the poets. Sexes similar. Length 15 in.

**NIGHTJAR.** Grey-brown colour pattern, mottled and streaked with various shades of brown and buff, creates an effective protective coloration, and it is difficult to detect when sitting. Length 10½ in.

# Index

## THE COMPLETE ART OF PRINTING AND ENLARGING

*By O. R. Croy*

Every kind of print and every modern printing process is explained: straightforward prints, elaborate enlargements, trick control, combination techniques, methods of montage and after-treatment at every level. A truly encyclopaedic volume handing out tested advice in every sentence and practical evidence for it in every picture. "One of those books which suffice for a lifetime," says the Press.
256 pp., 443 illus., 4th ed.　　　**Price 19/6**

## THE COLOUR BOOK OF PHOTOGRAPHY

*By Lucien Lorelle*

The beginner in colour photography will learn from this book that it needs little more care than black-and-white—and will be shown how and when to exercise that extra care to achieve success. A full account of colour photography on a practical level—in terms of pictures rather than of processes—abounding in useful facts and hints.
188 pp., 130 illus., 2nd ed.　　　**Price 12/6**

## 35 mm. PHOTO TECHNIQUE

*By H. S. Newcombe*

The established standard work on 35 mm. procedure: from the choice of equipment to the presentation of major prints. It translates the inter-play of all the technical factors involved into methods of common sense. This book easily answers any 35er's question; it is sound and lucid, convincing and self-contained.
328 pp., 148 illus., 9th ed.　　　**Price 17/6**

## TWIN LENS REFLEX COMPANION

*By H. S. Newcombe*

The modern twin-lens reflex is by far the most popular camera of the day. This book maps out its world and reveals how success is achieved in it. Ten outstanding American photographers, led by a British expert, lay down the rules, reveal their methods and prove their points. Conscientious, instructive and stimulating.
320 pp., 160 illus., 3rd ed.　　　**Price 17/6**

## THE LEICA WAY

*By Andrew Matheson*

A volume worthy of the Leica. Explains Leica design, details old and new Leica equipment, instructs in every Leica technique, covers all Leica subjects, records a wealth of Leica data, shows the best Leica photographs. The key to the Leica system, it is comprehensive, methodical and authoritative—yet straight all the time. The book for any Leica recruit to turn to. The technical Bible no Leica expert can afford to be without.
426 pp., 352 illus., 3rd ed.　　　**Price 21/-**

## THE ROLLEI WAY

*By L. A. Mannheim*

This book interprets photography, explores its possibilities, warns of its pitfalls, throughout in terms of the Rolleiflex and the Rolleicord. Even the more experienced Rollei photographers will find it a welcome senior companion as an unfailing source of specialized knowledge and exact information on Rollei equipment, accessories and materials. Yet it starts with the novice at the very beginning.

232 pp., 281 illus., 4th ed.　　　**Price 17/6**

## THE CONTAX WAY

*By H. Freytag*

Twenty years of experience went into this book. A master of the Contax tells how to use it and how every piece of Contax equipment adds to its supreme flexibility. A wealth of up-to-date information, superb photographs, penetrating diagrams and an inexhaustible mine of data answer every Contax owner's needs.
280 pp., 286 illus., 5th ed.　　　**Price 21/-**

## THE RETINA WAY

*By O. R. Croy*

Sets your fingers right on the controls of your Retina. Puts the whole Retina technique safely in your hands. Brings all the subjects of Retina photography within your easy reach. Your Retina will do more—much more—than you thought before having read this book—whatever type of pictures you are after.

304 pp., 236 illus., 5th ed.　　　**Price 21/-**

## LIGHTING FOR PORTRAITURE

*By W. Nurnberg*

Portrait lighting offers a greater variety of technique, range of style and scope of expression than any other camera work. This wealth of possibilities is broken down to a simple system of "how to do it" in this work. Its thoroughness, clarity and precision are as inimitable as the completeness of its illustrative material.
192 pp., 430 illus., 2nd ed.　　　**Price 17/6**

## LIGHTING FOR PHOTOGRAPHY

*By W. Nurnberg*

Where to put the lamps when taking portraits, groups, figure studies, still life, glass, metal or fabric. This book explains the principles, makes countless suggestions and shows over a hundred examples. It is a treasure trove of lighting ideas.

176 pp., 297 illus., 12th ed.　　　**Price 17/6**